The past two decades have witness
expositions of Ecclesiastes – and th
best of them. It follows the line of
compelling way. Its applications and reflections are cogent and telling, and the writing is characterized by grace and verve. Moreover, the questions found at the end of each chapter make this volume suitable for small-group Bible studies. Highly recommended.
D. A. Carson, *Research Professor of New Testament, Trinity Evangelical Divinity School, Deerfield, Illinois, and President of The Gospel Coalition*

David Gibson's expositions of Ecclesiastes are like Ecclesiastes itself: sometimes shocking, often tantalizing, always refreshing. He deftly combines serious stuff with a light touch, clear style and gospel relief. You will repeatedly run into 'think-stoppers'; he will make new grooves in your grey matter that weren't there before; and you will often admit, 'I wish I'd have thought to put it like that!' I think the writer of Ecclesiastes would be pleased with David's work.
Dale Ralph Davis, *formerly Professor of Old Testament, Reformed Theological Seminary, Jackson, Mississippi*

If Ecclesiastes is a book for our times, then *Destiny* is the book to unpack it. Beginning with the paradigm shift that embracing death is essential for life, I was intrigued from the start. Utterly counter to a modern world-view, the truths of Ecclesiastes are woven with ease into a narrative that rightly makes sense of why we are alive. Bold and beautiful in style, *Destiny* promises to jolt the mind and shake us out of our complacencies. I couldn't put it down!
Fiona McDonald, *Director of National Ministries, Scottish Bible Society*

Recently we worked through Ecclesiastes in our home groups at St George's, Poynton. Uniformly, people who had hitherto spurned it as 'too difficult' found themselves facing a Bible writer who seemed to be asking today's questions and giving timeless answers. Every reader of David Gibson's steady and reverent progress through the book will reap the same reward, along with wonderfully enhanced

understanding and rich insight into divine truth. Those who have benefited from David's work in the foundational book *From Heaven He Came and Sought Her* will rush to enjoy the same values here of profound scholarship and covetable clarity of presentation.
Alec Motyer, author and Bible expositor

destiny

destiny

Learning to live by preparing to die

David Gibson

INTER-VARSITY PRESS
36 Causton Street, London SW1P 4ST, England
Email: ivp@ivpbooks.com
Website: www.ivpbooks.com

© David Gibson, 2016

David Gibson has asserted his right under the Copyright, Designs and Patents Act, 1988, to be identified as Author of this work.

All rights reserved. No part of this publication may be reproduced, stored in a retrieval system, or transmitted, in any form or by any means, electronic, mechanical, photocopying, recording or otherwise, without the prior permission of the publisher or the Copyright Licensing Agency.

Unless otherwise indicated, Scripture quotations are taken from the Holy Bible, New International Version (Anglicized edition). Copyright © 1979, 1984, 2011 by Biblica (formerly International Bible Society). Used by permission of Hodder & Stoughton Publishers, an Hachette UK company. All rights reserved. 'NIV' is a registered trademark of Biblica (formerly International Bible Society). UK trademark number 1448790.

Scripture quotations from Ecclesiastes 11 in chapter 8 are from the NIV 1978 edition.

First published 2016

British Library Cataloguing-in-Publication Data
A catalogue record for this book is available from the British Library.

ISBN: 978–1–78359–285–2
eBook ISBN: 978–1–78359–521–1

Typeset in Great Britain by CRB Associates, Potterhanworth, Lincolnshire
Printed and bound in Great Britain by Ashford Colour Press Ltd, Gosport, Hampshire

Inter-Varsity Press publishes Christian books that are true to the Bible and that communicate the gospel, develop discipleship and strengthen the church for its mission in the world.

IVP originated within the Inter-Varsity Fellowship, now the Universities and Colleges Christian Fellowship, a student movement connecting Christian Unions in universities and colleges throughout Great Britain, and a member movement of the International Fellowship of Evangelical Students. Website: www.uccf.org.uk. That historic association is maintained, and all senior IVP staff and committee members subscribe to the UCCF Basis of Faith.

For Trinity Church, Aberdeen

*This is the evil in everything that happens under the sun:
The same destiny overtakes all.*
Ecclesiastes 9:3

*Nothing brings such pure peace and quiet joy at the close
as a well-lived past.*
James Russell Miller

Contents

	Preface	xi
	Acknowledgments	xiv
1	Let's pretend	1
2	Bursting the bubble	19
3	Doing time	36
4	Living a life less upwardly mobile	51
5	Looking up, listening in	68
6	Learning to love the limitations of life	81
7	From death to depth	97
8	Things to know when you don't know	112
9	One foot in the grave	126
10	Getting the point	147
	Notes	161

Preface

I am going to die. By the time you read these lines, I may even be dead.

It's not that I have a virulent disease or a terminal illness. A doctor has not pronounced on how I am going to die. I don't know when I will die. I just know I will. I am going to die, and so are you. But here is why I wrote this book: I am ready to die.

In his beautifully written memoir, *Hitch-22*, Christopher Hitchens quotes the words of the Scottish poet William Dunbar: 'The fear of death distresses me.' Hitchens comments, 'I would not trust anyone who had not felt something like it.'[1] I know what he means, and you probably do as well. There are certain ways in which we would rather not meet our end. I do find myself worrying about what would happen if my wife were to die, or one of my children, or others closest to me. But I myself am not afraid of dying. There is nothing about my own death, or the state of being dead, which distresses me.

I can understand if you share Hitchens' distrust and find this way of thinking rather odd, morbid even. But I would like to try to change your mind. I am convinced that only a proper perspective on death provides the true perspective on life.

Living in the light of your death will help you to live wisely and freely and generously. It will give you a big heart and open hands, and enable you to relish all the small things of life in deeply profound ways. Death can teach you the meaning of mirth. All this I have learned from Ecclesiastes, and the chapters of this book consist of reflections on that strangest of Old Testament books.

Ecclesiastes has changed my death. But it is an enigma. It has baffled scholars and pundits with its repeated refrain: 'Meaningless! Meaningless! Everything is meaningless!' In my opinion, part of the brilliance of Ecclesiastes is that it teaches us that life often slips through our fingers and eludes our comprehension by being itself elusive and perplexing. Is there a better way to explain how life can leave you scratching your head than by writing a book that leaves you doing the same? The message of the book is mirrored in the effect of the book.

Yet Ecclesiastes also makes a very simple point: life is complex and messy, sometimes brutally so, but there is a straightforward way to look at the mess. The end will put it all right. The end – when we stand before God as our Creator and Judge – will explain everything.

Left to our own devices, we tend to live life forwards. One day follows another and weeks turn into months and months into years. We do not know the future, but we plan and hope and dream of where we will be, and what we would like to be doing, and whom we might be with. We live forwards.

Ecclesiastes teaches us to live life backwards. It encourages us to take the one thing in the future that is certain – our death – and work backwards from that point into all the details and decisions and heartaches of our lives, and to think about them from the perspective of the end. It is the destination that makes sense of the journey. If we know for sure where we are heading, then we can know for sure what we need to do before we get there. Ecclesiastes invites us to let the end sculpt our priorities and goals, our greatest ambitions and our strongest desires.

I want to persuade you that only if you prepare to die can you really learn how to live.

Acknowledgments

Blaise Pascal said that the more intelligent a man is, the more originality he finds in others. That is my excuse for the number of people I have leaned on in different ways to bring this book to completion. Many of them don't even know it.

Nathan D. Wilson's *Death by Living* (Thomas Nelson, 2013) was published when I was halfway through my writing. I knew before opening his book that it might mean I never finished mine. It is an arresting treatment of a viewpoint I'm proud to share, but, with wit and elegance, Wilson shows how time is grace and generations are a gift, and in so doing lights up the landscape of a life well lived. Perhaps my work can trace a more expository line of thought to function as an uninvited companion to his. Certainly I hope all who read me also read him.

I am indebted, in a different way, to Iain Provan's commentary, *Ecclesiastes and Song of Songs* (Zondervan, 2001). He has produced that most endangered of species, a commentary immediately useful to preachers. Zack Eswine has followed his profound pastoral theology, *Sensing Jesus* (Crossway, 2012), with a similarly rich and thoughtful treatment of Ecclesiastes, *Recovering Eden* (P&R, 2014), and both have helped me here. Worthy of special mention as well are Craig Bartholomew's commentary (Baker, 2009), and the meditations by Douglas Wilson in *Joy at the End of the Tether* (Canon Press, 1999). Andrew Randall and the blog of Tim Challies introduced me to the writings of James Russell Miller (1840–1912), and the archivists at the Presbyterian Historical Society in Philadelphia helped me track down the source of his essay, which I quote in chapter 9.

Peter Dickson and I preached through Ecclesiastes together at High Church, Hilton in 2009. For that – and for more things than I can count – I owe him a very great deal. I am thankful for his permission to use some of his ideas in these chapters. I taught Ecclesiastes to Cornhill Scotland students in 2010 and benefited from their interaction and from the kindness of Bob Fyall and Edward Lobb. Some of my material first appeared in *The Pastor as Public Theologian: Reclaiming a Lost Vision* (Baker Academic, 2015), and I am grateful to both the publisher and to the editors, Owen Strachan and Kevin Vanhoozer, for permission to reproduce it here.

Thanks are due to Ken Morley and to David and Laura Muirhead for the stay at fabulous Downingford in Strathdon, which helped me to finish and provided refreshment. A cadre of friends, postgraduate students and colleagues read all or parts of the manuscript and helped to improve it substantially; others shouldered my responsibilities while I shirked them to write. I want to express my thanks to Taido Chino, Andrew Errington, John Ferguson, Nicola Fitch, Ian MacCormick, Andrew Randall, Andy and Cara Ritson, Ben Traynor, Drew Tulloch, Martin Westerholm and Adam Wilson.

I am especially grateful to my fellow elders at Trinity Church, Aberdeen – Simon Barker, Lawrie Fairns and David Macleod – and the Trustees of The Cruden Trust, for their support and care, which enabled writing time to be carved out of otherwise pressured time. It is a great joy to dedicate this book to the wonderful church family I am privileged to serve. Their encouragement, fortitude, vitality and love for Christ are a rich delight.

Sam Parkinson and Eleanor Trotter at IVP graciously granted a faraway contract, then patiently accepted further delays, and never once said that everything I told them was meaningless, meaningless.

To my wife Angela, my sons Archie and Samuel, and my daughters Ella and Lily: what can I say? You are the ones who helped me hear the Teacher of Ecclesiastes laughing as he shows how shoulders are meant for abundance and mayhem, not the weight of the world. You've always been laughing, and now we're in on the joke together. I can't remember not being so tired or ever so happy. I wish we could stay forever this young.

One day we will.

1

Let's pretend

'Preach the gospel. Die. Be forgotten.'
Nikolaus Ludwig von Zinzendorf

The words of the Teacher, son of David, king of Jerusalem:

'Meaningless! Meaningless!'
   says the Teacher.
'Utterly meaningless!
   Everything is meaningless.'
What do people gain from all their labours
   at which they toil under the sun?
Generations come and generations go,
   but the earth remains for ever.
The sun rises and the sun sets,
   and hurries back to where it rises.
The wind blows to the south
   and turns to the north;
round and round it goes,
      ever returning on its course.
All streams flow into the sea,
   yet the sea is never full.

To the place the streams come from,
  there they return again.
All things are wearisome,
  more than one can say.
The eye never has enough of seeing,
  nor the ear its fill of hearing.
What has been will be again,
  what has been done will be done again;
  there is nothing new under the sun.
Is there anything of which one can say,
  'Look! This is something new'?
It was here already, long ago;
  it was here before our time.
No one remembers the former generations,
  and even those yet to come
will not be remembered
  by those who follow them.
(Ecclesiastes 1:1–11)

The explosive gift

The development of imagination is one of the most intriguing things that happens as little toddlers begin to explore their world. Suddenly, in just a matter of weeks, the sitting room or garden in which the toddler plays becomes a zoo, a garage, a farm, a hospital, a palace, a tea party, a battlefield, a sports stadium. A world of 'let's pretend' opens up to inspire and to cultivate real understanding of the world. The toddler is ushered into new relationships and creative language by pretending to be someone they are not. If you manage to eavesdrop, you will hear all sorts of conversations as the toddler scolds and pleads, and says 'sorry' and 'thank you' to a host of imaginary friends.

But learning the difference between the pretend world and the real world can often be a confusing process. In the real shop you can't just buy whatever you want. In the real hospital people are actually in pain and the doctors can't always make everyone better. In the real world making amends is sometimes the hardest thing possible. Real tears take longer to dry.

The book of Ecclesiastes is one of God's gifts to help us live in the real world. It's a book in the Bible that gets under the radar of our thinking and acts like an incendiary device to explode our make-believe games and jolt us into realizing that everything is not as clean and tidy as the 'let's-pretend' world suggests.

Ecclesiastes is the words of 'the Teacher, son of David, king of Jerusalem',[1] and he begins with shock tactics. The very first thing he wants to tell us is that 'everything is meaningless', 'utterly meaningless'. If you want a reader to wake up and stop pretending about what life is like, that's a pretty good way to get their attention.

The meaning of 'meaningless'

Of course, to commence in such a direct and stark way poses its own problem. What does it mean to say everything is 'meaningless'?

I want to propose that many well-intended Bible translations have actually led us astray by translating the Hebrew word *hebel* as 'meaningless' in this context. We tend to read this word as if it's spoken by an undergraduate philosophy student who comes home after his first year of studies and confidently announces that the universe as we know it is pointless and life has no meaning. But that is not the Teacher's perspective. He will later make statements such as 'Better one handful with tranquillity / than two handfuls with toil' (4:6).

If one course of action is *better* than another, then clearly not everything is 'meaningless'.

In fact, the Hebrew word *hebel* is also accurately translated as 'breath' or 'breeze'. The Teacher is saying that everything is a mist, a vapour, a puff of wind, a bit of smoke. It's a common biblical idea:

> You have made my days a mere handbreadth;
>   the span of my years is as nothing before you.
> Everyone is but a breath [*hebel*],
>   even those who seem secure.
> Surely everyone goes around like a mere phantom;
>   in vain [*hebel*] they rush about, heaping up wealth
>   without knowing whose it will finally be.
> When you rebuke and discipline anyone for their sin,
>   you consume their wealth like a moth –
>   surely everyone is but a breath [*hebel*].
> (Psalm 39:5–6, 11)

> LORD, what are human beings that you care for them,
>   mere mortals that you think of them?
> They are like a breath [*hebel*];
>   their days are like a fleeting shadow.
> (Psalm 144:3–4)

The Teacher's portrayal of life is this: 'The merest of breaths . . . the merest of breaths. Everything is a breath.' He will take the rest of his book to unpack exactly what he means, but here are some ways to think about it.

Life is short
You know what happens when you blow out a candle. How long does the puff of smoke last? You can smell it and see it.

It's very real. But it is also transient, temporary, and vanishes quickly. It comes and goes without a permanent impact or a lasting impression on the world.

You have found yourself saying exactly what you used to hear older people saying all the time: 'Time flies the older you get.' Your grandparents say it's as if they blinked and now here they are in an old person's body. We are born, we live, we die, and it all happens so quickly. Nothing seems to last. 'Charm is deceptive, and beauty is fleeting [*hebel*]' (Proverbs 31:30). Joan Collins said that the problem with beauty is that it's like being born rich and then becoming poor.

The book of Ecclesiastes is a meditation on what it means for our lives to be like a whisper spoken in the wind: here one minute, and carried away for ever the next.

Life is elusive

But the smoke in front of your eyes is not just transient, it is also elusive. Try to grab the smoke, put a bit in your pocket and keep it for later. You can't get your hands on it. It is a real, physical thing, and yet it dodges your fingers as soon as they get near it; your very attempt to get hold of it blows air at the smoke and speeds its disappearance.

Ecclesiastes is a meditation on how life seems to elude our grasp in terms of lasting significance. If we try to gain control of the world and our lives by what we can understand and by what we can do, we find that the control we seek eludes us.

Consider knowledge and understanding. In some measure we can understand how the world works, but why does it always rain on the days when you don't bring your umbrella? Why is the queue you don't join in the supermarket always quicker than the one you do? Why do you feel low, even when you can't really put your finger on a specific cause? Why do people you know and love die young or suffer long-term ill health while the dictator lives in prosperity into his old age?

Or consider what we do with our lives. We can pour our whole life into something, and it might succeed, or it might fail. You might land the big job in the city and the bank might go bust the next month – you never know. How much control do you really have over whether your job is secure, or how healthy you will be, or what will happen to interest rates and house prices, over whom you will meet and what you will be doing in ten years' time?

Not long ago I was building sandcastles on the beach with my daughter. With some success we built a large castle, dug a moat around it and surrounded it with smaller castles and turrets decorated with shells. She was proud of her work and we enjoyed being absorbed in our task. But eventually – and to her great surprise – we had to retreat as the tide encroached and the waves engulfed our handiwork. The foaming water returned our project to a knobbly patch of ordinary beach. How long do sandcastles last? And how much control do we have over the castle we have constructed? We build for a short time only, and always subject to forces beyond our control. That is what our lives are like. Instead of sand and sea, the Bible uses grass and wind to make exactly this point:

> The life of mortals is like grass,
>   they flourish like a flower of the field;
> the wind blows over it and it is gone,
>   and its place remembers it no more.
> (Psalm 103:15–16)

These pictures hit home. When we consider the brevity of our lives set against the millennia of the earth, we know that what the Teacher says is true. Except, of course, in everyday life we pretend it isn't. We imagine we will live for ever, or at the very least that someone else will get cancer, not us. We think our lives are built with granite, not sand. We pretend we're in control. We imagine that we can make a difference in the world and accomplish things of lasting significance. After all, that's why we go to work each day. It's also why we have a mid-life crisis when we look back and see that who we are and what we've done doesn't seem to amount to very much.

And so Ecclesiastes sets out to demolish our pretence by confronting us with reality. The Teacher begins the process with a question:

> What do people gain from all their labours
>   at which they toil under the sun?
> (Ecclesiastes 1:3)

This question is the key to the opening section of the book. Everything else that follows in verses 4–11 is intended as the answer. The responses to questions are often implicit and indirect in Ecclesiastes because it is part of the Bible's wisdom literature. This kind of writing mixes bald, direct statements (1:2) with indirect analogies and pictorial representations (1:4–8), since the aim of the writing is to reflect on the complex reality of the world as we find it.

Wisdom literature asks, what does it mean to fear the Lord in the world the Lord has made? Along with Job, Proverbs and Song of Songs, Ecclesiastes is a meditation on what it means to be alive in a world that God made and called good, yet which has also gone so very wrong, often in catastrophic ways. The Teacher experiments with everything around him, and similarly wants us to reflect on our experience of the world. Look at your life and what's happening to you. What does that tell you about life in general? How should we make sense of it? Can we ever make sense of it? Wisdom literature uses proverbs and pithy sayings, riddles and provocation, question and answer, prose and poetry, to force us to look at things from a different angle. Its aim is to 'wound from behind'.[2] Like a punch in the back, it makes painful points we didn't see coming and which leave us blinking in surprise.

That's exactly what is happening here. The implied answer to the question of verse 3 is 'nothing'. From a life full of labour and toil under the sun, people gain absolutely nothing. The word 'gain' conveys the idea of something left over, remaining at the end. It refers to 'the human desire to show a profit, to be in the black, whether financially or otherwise'.[3]

This is what's at stake in the question of verse 3: at the end of my life, what will the surplus be? What will I leave behind that will count as a lasting monument to all my effort?

The Teacher provides the answer by painting an incredibly stark picture. He sketches humankind's place on the canvas of the entire universe to show, in graphic terms, just how and why there is nothing to be gained. I leave only one thing behind, and that's the earth I used to live on, remaining right where it was when I first arrived, only now it spins without me. My life will come and go. If I leave children in the world to carry on my legacy, they themselves are simply part of the generations who will come and go, and all they will leave behind is the universe carrying on as before. We haven't altered the cosmic merry-go-round. Nothing we do changes the fact that we labour and toil and then die, and the earth just stays there.

Everything is a breath, our lives the merest of breaths.

Life is repetitive

The Teacher pictures the momentary and elusive nature of human life with a beautiful rhythmic pattern to his poetry. Read verses 4–10 aloud and feel the lyrical tilt with its tidal ebb and flow. That's the point. Everything either goes round and round, or comes and goes; it rises and sets; what has been will be again; what has been done will be done again; what is present will soon be past.

In verses 5–8 the Teacher focuses on a threefold pattern in the world that is matched by a threefold pattern in human experience. The activities of sun, wind and water follow the same course as the activities of speaking, seeing and hearing. The point is that the world itself doesn't seem to go or get anywhere, for everything is cyclical rather than linear, so why should humans get anywhere?

The sun chases its tail. The wind goes to the south and comes back round again to the north. Streams flow into the sea, and the water evaporates, and then streams flow into the sea again and it is never full. So is the world, and so it will always be. So is humankind, and so we will always be. People are like the insatiable sea. Just as water pours into the ocean again and again without ever filling it, so the things of the world pour into human beings via their eyes and ears and back out through their mouths, and yet they never reach a point of complete satisfaction:

> The massive reality of creation thus critiques the aspirations of all those tiny mortal beings who stand within creation as transient creatures. There is no reason to assume that individuals should 'gain' from their toil when creation as a whole does not.[4]

The experience of observing constant motion without lasting achievement is so wearisome that no amount of speech can catalogue it. The eye 'never reaches the point that it cannot take in more, nor does the ear become so filled with sound that it cannot accept any more impulses from the outside world'.[5] Humans never finally think, 'This is it. I'm full. I have seen it all, said it all and heard it all. I have given out and taken in all that I can.'

This language could, of course, be extremely positive. Taken on their own, these words about the limitless capacities of the human body might point to endless potential, healthy curiosity and childlike wonder at the world in which we live. There is always so much to see and hear. But they are followed by perhaps the most famous words in the book of Ecclesiastes:

> What has been will be again,
>   what has been done will be done again;
> there is nothing new under the sun.
>
> (verse 9)

The Teacher's perspective is this: humans long to come across something in their lives that will break the constant repetitive cycle, something to say or see or hear which will be truly new and therefore significant – but there is nothing. No such thing exists. Whatever we see and hear has already been and gone, covered by the sands of time and simply rolling round again, perhaps in a different guise but fundamentally the same as before.

In *Hamlet's BlackBerry: A Practical Philosophy for Building a Good Life in the Digital Age*, William Powers argues that our constant connection to digital media and screen-based forms of communication is suffocating our ability to be people of substantial depth. Perhaps if anything in the world is new, then surely it's our technology, with rapidly evolving ways of sending messages and forming virtual communities, such that we seem to be presented with new challenges for what technology means for us as persons. Not so, according to Powers: 'Though we barely realize it, every day we use connective tools that were invented thousands of years ago.' He consults seven thinkers throughout world history who each 'understood the essential human urge to connect and were unusually thoughtful about the "screen equivalents" of their respective epochs'.[6] Human beings have wrestled throughout the ages with constantly changing forms of communication. There is already a rich seam of reflection on what human beings need to preserve about themselves as they interact with others. What seems new is in fact old. Hamlet used the BlackBerry of his day.[7]

The point Powers makes about the digital age applies to everything under the sun. A new government is still a government, and we're all familiar with those. A revolution heralds a new era, and we've seen it all before. A new baby is still a baby, and the world has always been full of them. Even landing on the moon is still a form of adventure and exploration that has been with us since humans have walked the earth. Indeed, space travel is a good example of precisely the Teacher's point. He doesn't mean no 'new' things are ever invented in the world, for clearly that is not true. He means there is nothing new we can ever discover to break the cycle and so satisfy us. When we conquer our solar system, humanity will then try to conquer the galaxy beyond it. We never have our fill, and that basic human impulse which led us to space in the first place 'was here already, long ago; it was here before our time' (1:10). There is nothing new about humanity in the unfolding of all our progress.

Remember the Teacher's aim. He is showing that at the end of the day human beings gain nothing from all their toil under the sun. There's no surplus because they are never full enough to have something left over. There's no gain because the universe itself is cyclical and everything that is comes and goes. There's no profit because whatever is, has already been. If there's 'nothing new under the sun', what's the point in toiling to make or find or leave something new? It simply can't be done.

You gain nothing from grinding your fingers to the bone, because the world will go on impervious to what you've done, and it will not remember you anyway. It will not even remember the children we are yet to have (1:11). How's that for perspective when your daughter graduates from university and your son clinches that multi-million-dollar deal?

No one will remember them.

Prepare to die

The Teacher has answered his own question by pointing to the cyclical comings and goings of the world. His answer is that people do not gain from their labour and toil because ultimately they are going to die and be forgotten. Life stretches ahead of the young employee with dreams of a fulfilling career and a happy family; but it will all come and go. She is going to die and will not be remembered.

Many interpreters of Ecclesiastes suggest the Teacher is simply presenting something that is true only if life is lived without God. They understand the phrase 'under the sun' to signify the secularist's perspective. If we consider life without God in the frame and look at the world as we see it, that is, under the sun, then there is no alternative but to say that everything is a mere breath. The Teacher, however, wants us to know that 'under the sun' is not all there is. And so we may well want to ask: surely the Christian way of looking at life is different? If I'm a follower of the Lord Jesus, doesn't that change everything?

Well, it is true that knowing Christ does provide a whole new angle – the true angle – on what it means to be alive. We will see how Ecclesiastes points us to this. It's certainly true that for the Teacher the world under the sun is not all there is, and he has things to say that will radically alter our perspective on this life.

But in the poetry that opens his book the Teacher is not commenting on what life is like without Christ. He is not saying this repetitive roundabout is what life is like from a secularist perspective. This is not what the world feels like from the viewpoint of existential nihilism, or postmodern navel-gazing. It's just what the world is like. It's reality. It's the same for everyone, Christian or non-Christian, adherent or atheist: we each live under the sun.

In fact, it's probably better to see that phrase as a temporal marker more than a spatial marker: 'In Scripture, the sun is a marker of time (Gen. 1:14) and the phrase "under the sun" . . . refers to a *now* rather than a *there*.'[8] It's a way of saying that for as long as the earth lasts, in this period of time, this is how things are. This side of eternity, life is a breath. We do the same things over and over again in a world repeating itself over and over again, and then we die, only to be followed by our children who will do the same things in the same way and then meet the same end.

Being a Christian doesn't stop this being true. Rather, it should make us the first to stop pretending that it isn't true. That is the Teacher's aim. It may not make perfect sense to us yet, but he is carefully laying the foundations for the main argument of his book: only preparing to die will teach us how to live. And part of establishing that argument is the very simple point of 1:1–11. In these days, under the sun, it is unavoidably true that we live in a world where we will soon be dead.

Learn to live

The Teacher wants us to let the reality of our death sink into our bones and lodge itself deep in our hearts. But that's because he's writing a book about what it means to live. He wants the consequences of our fast-approaching disappearance from the earth to work their way out into all the realities of the way we see the world and the way we view ourselves within that world. The single question that animates him is this: if we won't live for ever, or even long enough to make a lasting difference to the world, how then should we live?

It takes the whole of Ecclesiastes to answer that question, and I want to unpack it in the successive chapters of this book. The argument is cumulative, and we need to allow the Teacher to make his case bit by bit, like an artist painting on a canvas.

At the outset, 1:1–11 sketches a very basic point: accepting death is the first step in learning to live. Wise people simply accept that they are going to die. As Douglas Wilson puts it, 'A wise believer is a man who knows the length of his tether.'[9] This point may seem so obvious as to be simplistic. But in fact, it's highly significant when we stop and think about how much energy we devote to not accepting it.

The reality is, we spend our lives trying to escape the constraints of our created condition. Opening our eyes to this is a significant breakthrough. To be human is to be a creature, and to be a creature is to be finite. We are not God. We are not in control and we will not live for ever. We will die. But we avoid this reality by playing 'let's pretend'.

Let's pretend that if we get the promotion, or see our church grow, or bring up good children, we'll feel significant and leave a lasting legacy behind us. Let's pretend that if we change jobs, or emigrate to the sun, we won't experience the humdrum tedium and ordinariness of life. Let's pretend that if we move house, we'll be happier and will never want to move again. Let's pretend that if we end one relationship and start a new one, we won't ever feel trapped. Let's pretend that if we were married, or weren't married, we would be content. Let's pretend that if we had more money, we would be satisfied. Let's pretend that if we get through this week's pile of washing and dirty nappies and shopping lists and school runs and busy evenings, next week will be quieter. Let's pretend that time is always on our side to do the things we want to do and become the people we want to be. Let's pretend we can break the cycle of repetition and finally arrive in a world free from weariness.

We long for change in a world of permanent repetition and we dream of how to interrupt it. We long for lives of permanence in a world of constant change and we strive to achieve it. We spend our lives aligning our better selves with a different future that we envisage as more rewarding. And in it all we are simply trying to make permanent what is not meant to be permanent (us), and by constant change we are trying to control what is not meant to be controlled (the world). The seasons and natural cycles of the world are content to come and go, but we sweat and toil to make believe that it will not be so with us.

Ecclesiastes urges us to put this behind us once and for all and adopt a better way of thinking. Stop playing 'let's pretend' and instead let history and the created world be our teachers. Think about the generations who lived before us. Look at the tides and the seasons and the patterns which God has stitched into the very fabric of creation. Things repeat themselves over and over and over again, and so it is time to learn that life has a repetitiveness built into it which we are not meant to try to escape. The very rhythms of the world are a pointer to what it means to be part of the created order as a human being.

Stop thinking that meaning and happiness and satisfaction reside in novelty. What is new is not really new, and what feels new will soon feel old.

C. S. Lewis captured the essence of this point in his book, *The Screwtape Letters*. A senior devil, Screwtape, is writing to his junior devil nephew, Wormwood, with advice on how to get Christians to turn away from the Enemy (God). Screwtape counsels Wormwood on humanity's constant desire to experience something new:

> The horror of the Same Old Thing is one of the most valuable passions we have produced in the human heart – an endless source of heresies in religion, folly in counsel, infidelity in marriage, and inconstancy in friendship.[10]

God has made change and newness pleasurable to human beings. But, says Screwtape, because God does not want his creatures 'to make change, any more than eating, an end in itself, He has balanced the love of change in them by a love of permanence'.[11] Change and constancy are the two balancing weights on the see-saw of human experience, and God has given humanity the means to enjoy both of them by patterning the world with rhythm. We love the fact that springtime feels *new*; we love the fact that it is springtime *again*. And the devil goes to work right at this point.

Screwtape explains:

> Now just as we pick out and exaggerate the pleasure of eating to produce gluttony, so we pick out this natural pleasantness of change and twist it into a demand for absolute novelty. This demand is entirely our workmanship. If we neglect our duty, men will be not only contented but transported by the mixed novelty and familiarity of snowdrops *this* January, sunrise *this* morning,

plum pudding *this* Christmas. Children, until we have taught them better, will be perfectly happy with a seasonal round of games in which conkers succeed hopscotch as regularly as autumn follows summer. Only by our incessant efforts is the demand for infinite, or unrhythmical, change kept up.[12]

This is exactly what the Teacher wants us to spot. Where we are unsatisfied with the rhythmical repetition of our lives, it is because we are pretending that things should not be like this for us as human beings. To want infinite change – in other words, to 'gain' something – is to want to escape the confines of ordinary existence and somehow arrive in a world where, on the one hand, repetition does not occur and, on the other, permanence for our lives does. But neither is possible. As we search for something new under the sun, so we are searching for absolute novelty, and it does not exist: 'The pleasure of novelty is by its very nature more subject than any other to the law of diminishing returns.'[13]

When you think that at last you've made a decisive change in your circumstances, you will soon want to change something else. Whatever it is you think you've gained, it will soon vanish from the earth like morning mist, and you along with it too. Part of learning to live is simply accepting this. One day you will be dead and gone and the world will go on, probably without even remembering you. A hundred years after your death the chances are, no one will ever know you lived.

If this depresses you, then keep reading. There's still a lot to learn. But if it cracks a wry smile on your face, you're halfway to happiness. For the Teacher is going to show us what we should, and should not, expect out of life. He is not just saying there's no gain after we've chased the wind; he will insist there's no need for the chase in the first place.

There is no gain to be had under the sun, and that's precisely the point.

None need be sought.

Questions for discussion or personal reflection

1. What are your impressions of the book of Ecclesiastes?
2. Explain the meaning of 'meaningless' in Ecclesiastes in your own words.
3. List three things you would like to change about your life, and three things you would like to stay the same.
4. Can you think of instances when you felt you had 'gained', only to find that in time you were dissatisfied again?
5. How can it be liberating, rather than frustrating, to know that life is repetitive?
6. Do you find the message of this first chapter depressing or promising?

2

Bursting the bubble

*'Our excesses are the best clues to our own poverty,
and our best way of concealing it from ourselves.'*
Adam Philips, quoted in *The Times*

I, the Teacher, was king over Israel in Jerusalem. I applied my mind to study and to explore by wisdom all that is done under the heavens. What a heavy burden God has laid on mankind! I have seen all the things that are done under the sun; all of them are meaningless, a chasing after the wind.

What is crooked cannot be straightened;
    what is lacking cannot be counted.

I said to myself, 'Look, I have increased in wisdom more than anyone who has ruled over Jerusalem before me; I have experienced much of wisdom and knowledge.' Then I applied myself to the understanding of wisdom, and also of madness and folly, but I learned that this, too, is a chasing after the wind.

For with much wisdom comes much sorrow;
    the more knowledge, the more grief.

I said to myself, 'Come now, I will test you with pleasure to find out what is good.' But that also proved to be meaningless. 'Laughter,' I said, 'is madness. And what does pleasure accomplish?' I tried cheering myself with wine, and embracing folly – my mind still guiding me with wisdom. I wanted to see what was good for people to do under the heavens during the few days of their lives.

I undertook great projects: I built houses for myself and planted vineyards. I made gardens and parks and planted all kinds of fruit trees in them. I made reservoirs to water groves of flourishing trees. I bought male and female slaves and had other slaves who were born in my house. I also owned more herds and flocks than anyone in Jerusalem before me. I amassed silver and gold for myself, and the treasure of kings and provinces. I acquired male and female singers, and a harem as well – the delights of a man's heart. I became greater by far than anyone in Jerusalem before me. In all this my wisdom stayed with me.

I denied myself nothing my eyes desired;
    I refused my heart no pleasure.
My heart took delight in all my labour,
    and this was the reward for all my toil.
Yet when I surveyed all that my hands had done
    and what I had toiled to achieve,
everything was meaningless, a chasing after the wind;
    nothing was gained under the sun.
Then I turned my thoughts to consider wisdom,
    and also madness and folly.
What more can the king's successor do
    than what has already been done?
I saw that wisdom is better than folly,
    just as light is better than darkness.
The wise have eyes in their heads,
    while the fool walks in the darkness;

but I came to realise
> that the same fate overtakes them both.

Then I said to myself,
> 'The fate of the fool will overtake me also.
> What then do I gain by being wise?'

I said to myself,
> 'This too is meaningless.'

For the wise, like the fool, will not be long remembered;
> the days have already come when both have been forgotten.

Like the fool, the wise too must die!

So I hated life, because the work that is done under the sun was grievous to me. All of it is meaningless, a chasing after the wind. I hated all the things I had toiled for under the sun, because I must leave them to the one who comes after me. And who knows whether that person will be wise or foolish? Yet they will have control over all the fruit of my toil into which I have poured my effort and skill under the sun. This too is meaningless. So my heart began to despair over all my toilsome labour under the sun. For a person may labour with wisdom, knowledge and skill, and then they must leave all they own to another who has not toiled for it. This too is meaningless and a great misfortune. What do people get for all the toil and anxious striving with which they labour under the sun? All their days their work is grief and pain; even at night their minds do not rest. This too is meaningless.

A person can do nothing better than to eat and drink and find satisfaction in their own toil. This too, I see, is from the hand of God, for without him, who can eat or find enjoyment? To the person who pleases him, God gives wisdom, knowledge and happiness, but to the sinner he gives the task of gathering and storing up wealth to hand it over to the one who pleases God. This too is meaningless, a chasing after the wind.
(Ecclesiastes 1:12 – 2:26)

The Teacher and the travellers

In this world, those who follow Jesus Christ never find a permanent home. We find peace with God through Christ, and there is rest for the weary and burdened. But the gospel does not lead us into a settled life of contented ease. This has always been true of God's family. The writer to the Hebrews says about Abraham,

> By faith he made his home in the promised land like a stranger in a foreign country; he lived in tents, as did Isaac and Jacob, who were heirs with him of the same promise. For he was looking forward to the city with foundations, whose architect and builder is God.
> (Hebrews 11:9–10)

To be a believer is to be a stranger and a misfit. We have no permanent roots in this world, and no sense of real belonging here. We are travelling through.

Or are we?

People who follow Jesus often lose sight of the world to come. We become resident Christians rather than nomadic Christians. We become fully integrated in this world rather than viewing ourselves as passing through, and we do this by living as if our greatest treasures are the here and now. We display our sense of permanence by our lifestyle choices: the homes we live in, the money we spend, the churches we build, the investments we pursue and the priorities we live for. We hold the good things of this world too tightly, and lavish our affections on them too freely. We strive and strain for the same kind of gain as everyone else around us.

Jesus knew this would always be the temptation for his disciples. He warns us:

> Do not store up for yourselves treasures on earth, where moths and vermin destroy, and where thieves break in and steal. But store up for yourselves treasures in heaven, where moths and vermin do not destroy, and where thieves do not break in and steal. For where your treasure is, there your heart will be also. (Matthew 6:19–21)

And to stop us doing the wrong kind of storing, and to help us begin to do the right kind of storing, God has given us the book of Ecclesiastes.

In his first eleven verses the Teacher taught how the world itself shows there is no lasting gain in all our human toiling. He sought to end the games we play about the permanent significance of our lives. It was an argument from the brute fact of nature. But now the Teacher is going to mount an argument from bitter experience. He continues his demolition job by bursting bubbles. The bubbles he seeks to destroy are the very things that his readers might want to point to as the best counter-arguments against his case. It is one thing to say in general terms that 'all things are wearisome' (1:8), but quite another to maintain the argument in the face of specific test cases. What about having fun, contributing to society and building wealth? What about being wise? Is there really nothing to be gained from a life well spent in those pursuits? Does the Teacher honestly expect us to believe that all of these things are futile attempts to shepherd the wind? In a word, yes.

The Teacher will argue that wisdom, pleasure, work and possessions are very often the bubbles we live in to insulate ourselves from reality. And his needle, the sharp point he uses to burst the bubbles, is death. It is the great reality facing every human being as they go about their business on earth. Death is the one ultimate certainty that we erase from our minds and busy ourselves to avoid facing.

In this section, however, a very surprising shaft of light begins to break into this seemingly depressing thesis. Far from being something that makes life in the present completely pointless, future death is a light God shines on the present to change it. Death can radically enable us to enjoy life. By relativizing all that we do in our days under the sun, death can change us from people who want to control life for gain into people who find deep joy in receiving life as a gift. This is the main message of Ecclesiastes in a nutshell: *life in God's world is gift, not gain.*[1]

Here the Teacher begins to unpack that message by showing how he pursued gain in the world and what he realized at the end of his quest. When all was said and done, he was left staring at the cold hard fact of life's brutal emptiness. And yet his conclusion is ultimately positive and profound: 'The gift of God does not make this meaninglessness go away; the gift of God makes this vanity enjoyable.'[2]

We'll look at this section from three different angles to see how he arrives at that point.

1 The great human pursuit

When I was growing up, there were adverts on television for Hamlet cigars. Incredibly, they were recently listed as the eighth greatest advert of all time! There was a recurring pattern to the adverts of some poor man trying to achieve something which went horribly wrong each time. No matter how hard he tried, it would always miscarry. The humour of the adverts lay in watching him fall on his face again and again, until he resigned himself to failure and simply lit up his cigar. Cue the tag line: 'Happiness is a cigar called Hamlet.'

The adverts were a stroke of genius. They made us laugh so that all our defences were lowered. They showed us what we know to be true – life is messy and complicated and doesn't always work, and sometimes the best thing to do is just to accept it. They dared to tell us what every advert on TV is telling us: if you have this product, you will be happy. Happiness is here, with this aroma. Shut out all the troubles of life and the world, get this and you'll be happy. Quite simply, the adverts worked because happiness is what we live for.

Blaise Pascal said,

> All men seek happiness. This is without exception. Whatever different means they use, they all tend to this end. The cause of some going to war, and of others avoiding it, is the same desire in both – to be happy. This is the motive of every action of every man, even of those who hang themselves.[3]

Just about everything you've done so far today was to make yourself happy. You fed yourself. You stayed in the shower a bit longer because the kids were fighting downstairs. You dressed yourself. If you can, for the rest of the day you will do what makes you happy.

What we long for and live for is happiness, on the surface of our lives and at the deepest level of our lives. In all our varied pursuits – earning a living, finding a spouse, raising good children, having fun, keeping fit – we exhibit a common desire to be happy in what we do. We do not simply exist, suspended motionless in time. We shape and change the world and seek to control it. We plan and dream about our individual lives. We live with a purpose, towards a specific end, and we have a goal: to be happy.

The Teacher in Ecclesiastes is the same as us. He set out to explore 'all that is done under the heavens' (1:13) and he was determined 'to find out what is good' (2:1). In 2:3 he tells us that he 'wanted to see what was good for people to do under heaven during the few days of their lives'. His was a quest for satisfaction and meaning in life, and he pursued it by giving himself to wisdom, comedy, pleasure, alcohol, projects and possessions. As he did so, he held happiness in his hands – and then felt it slip through his fingers like water and vanish down the plughole. For ever.

These verses are the video diary of his adventure through life. First stop is Jerusalem University in 1:16–18. He studies and grows in wisdom. He learns from every professor and passes all his exams. He studies philosophy. He begins to understand how and why he understands. He studies the opposites of sanity and wisdom – madness and folly – to see what light they shed on understanding. All combine to be 'a chasing after the wind' (1:17). He learns so much and yet his heart aches like the man who knows nothing (1:18). Degree certificates line his study walls, but his tears are the same as the person working on the street who never even went to school.

'If ignorance is bliss,' wrote the teacher on the boy's school report, 'then this pupil is going to be the happiest person in the world.' We believe, of course, that the opposite is true. We are sure education can save us from all our ills and place us on the road to happiness. The Teacher shows us that this particular pursuit is as old as the hills. Get into the best schools, study hard, achieve the best results, learn and learn and learn, get up the ladder and you'll go far. Aim at the top and the sun will shine. Join the academic professionals and you will surely soar on the new heights of your knowledge. It is not so, says the Teacher. The more I knew, the sadder I became.

In the opening verses of chapter 2, the Teacher runs out of university to try a new approach. Let's hit the town, buy a ticket and watch a comedian. The expensive wine bars line the streets, and he sits outside in the sun savouring glass after glass. Life is short; I should enjoy myself. Live for today, shrug my shoulders, be happy. Why worry about life? These verses are the stuff of the fridge magnet and the bumper sticker. Forget it all, enjoy yourself and laugh.

Have you ever read the autobiography of a comedian? They are so often among the loneliest and saddest people in the world. Our national pastimes, for all their pleasure and fun, for all their creativity, are, for most people, simply a means of anaesthetizing themselves against the pain of reality. Whether you are at the more sophisticated end of the scale with art, music and fine wine, or whether you are watching a bawdy stand-up comic in the back room of a grotty pub, with the football blaring in one ear and the jukebox in the other, does it solve much?

Suddenly we turn another corner and the Teacher now becomes industrious (2:4). Perhaps work, management, projects, getting things done, maybe this is the way to go? Could it be this is where happiness dwells? Discipline, goals, finance, building and farming. Let's become general manager of the royal estate and chief executive for the parks and gardens department. Let's welcome responsibility and achieve great things. Why, my name may even be on a plaque one day if I get going and stick at it.

Next, power comes his way. And money, and of course sex – as much sex as a wealthy king could ever dream of. He is a man of influence at last. He is undoubtedly an A-list celebrity and secure at the top of the Forbes Rich List. Everything he wants, he has immediately. He loves life, and lives like no one has lived before.

This is the stuff of secret dreams. Fame and fortune, the sky is the limit and he seems to have reached it. Yet when he gets there, stands back and surveys his empire, it is all quite pointless, meaningless, a chasing after the wind (2:11). He has actually gained nothing. Thus says the man who owned everything. He discovered that although we pursue happiness in every corner of our lives, in the same corners lurks the darkness of diminishing returns. In the end, achievements and pleasures do not last. Everything is ephemeral. Happiness is a vanishing vapour. All our bubbles burst eventually.

2 The permanent human problem

As the Teacher hunts happiness in all the endeavours of life, clouds gather on the horizon to thwart his ambitions. He discovers that he cannot make the world different from how it actually is (1:15). He finds that a lot of learning exposes one to the complexity of life in a way that can be unbearable. Iain Provan recounts the tale from his university days of seeing an exceptional student, a philosophy major, sitting with a bottle of vodka in his hand rhythmically banging his head against a wall at a party.[4] And the Teacher, after all his projects and possessions and pleasures have run their course, realizes he is left with only sandcastles on the beach (2:11).

But each of these struggles is eclipsed by the one great shadow which has been encroaching all the way through this section. These troubles are not the source of the Teacher's ultimate perplexity in life. His greatest problem is death:

> The wise have eyes in their heads,
>   while the fool walks in the darkness;
> but I came to realise
>   that the same fate overtakes them both.
> (2:14)

Death stalks both the wise and the foolish. Do what they will with their lives, and do it differently, in time they will be indistinguishable:

> For the wise, like the fool, will not be long remembered;
>> the days have already come when both have been forgotten.
> Like the fool, the wise too must die!
> (2:16)

Throughout his lifelong experiment in ultimate meaning, the Teacher has not been living like a fool. Even cheering himself with wine and embracing folly was a studied exercise in the attempt to discover happiness (2:3). He didn't take leave of his senses. All along he knew what he was doing. Yet now he realizes that even living wisely in this way will not stop him being placed in a box in the ground, just like the village idiot.

It is the reality of death which alters the Teacher's perspective on all the achievements of his life. It slowly dawns on him that all his possessions will be left to someone else – and although *he* was wise, what's to say that his riches aren't going to fall in the lap of a fool (2:18–19)? We have returned to the agony of chapter 1. It is the people who follow us who will have control over all our toil and effort. Perhaps they will develop it. Perhaps they will destroy it. But either way, we will be dead and gone and soon forgotten. So what does that mean for all we have achieved? If there's no gain, why bother with anything?

If this sounds too bleak and pessimistic, I suspect it's because you haven't reflected at length on the brevity of life. If you haven't ever wondered why it matters what you do, given that one day you will be a forgotten nobody, then you haven't thought much about the reality of death. When we sit down and try to face it head-on, then the Teacher's words begin to bore into our skulls. 'What do people get for all the toil and anxious striving with which they labour under the sun?' (2:22). Not a lot, is the honest answer.

We are easily diverted from wrestling with questions like this. As Iain Provan comments, this section of Ecclesiastes 'is a sobering account of the relentless anxiety of the materialist who lives under the shadow of unavoidable death'.[5] Persistent angst is what sets in when you stare at all that the grave takes from us so ruthlessly. But who wants to think about the fact that we are going to die, let alone actually prepare for it in a deliberate way? Blaise Pascal argued, 'As men have not been able to cure death, misery, or ignorance, they have taken to not thinking about them so as to become happy.'[6] We refuse to think about these things by filling our lives with other things. Famously, Pascal went as far as suggesting that 'the sole cause of man's unhappiness is that he does not know how to stay quietly in his room'.[7] He believed that

> Nothing is so unbearable for a man as to be in complete repose, without passions, without business, without distraction, without application. Then he feels his nothingness, his abandonment, his insufficiency, his dependence, his impotence, his emptiness. Incontinent from the depths of his soul there will arise boredom, melancholy, sadness, sorrow, spite, despair.[8]

Distraction and diversion are what we use to console ourselves in the face of our miseries and confusions:

> Man is obviously made for thinking. Therein lies all his dignity and his merit; and his whole duty is to think as he ought. Now the order of thought is to begin with ourselves, and with our author and our end. Now what does the world think about? Never about that, but about dancing, playing the lute, singing, writing verse, tilting at the ring, etc., and becoming king, without thinking what it means to be a king or a man.[9]

If we cannot feel what the Teacher feels, it may be because we have given ourselves wholesale to a repertoire of diversions that distract us from addressing ultimate questions about our mortality. In Pascal's day, the diversions consisted of hunting, games, gambling and other such amusements. In our day, we are submerged beneath an abundance of trivia in our fully wired, always-connected, completely digitized world of social media and limitless sources of entertainment. The Teacher would not be negative about any of these things in themselves. He would simply ask us if we can cope with looking death in the eye, or whether we are trying to live in bubbles we think will never burst. The reality is that if death doesn't inform the way we live, then death is something we are pretending doesn't exist. As Peter Kreeft puts it in his explanations of Pascal:

> If you are typically modern, your life is like a mansion with a terrifying hole right in the middle of the living-room floor. So you paper over the hole with a very busy wallpaper pattern to distract yourself. You find a rhinoceros in the middle of your house. The rhinoceros is wretchedness and death. How in the world can you hide a rhinoceros? Easy: cover it with a million mice. Multiple diversions.[10]

The permanent human problem is that death comes to us all. None of us is permanent and nothing we do is permanent. We are going to die.

So far in his book the Teacher has sought to make us put away our distractions and confronted us with this truth head-on. Now – and only now – are we ready to receive his first shafts of light.

3 The true human perspective

Throughout this section the writer of Ecclesiastes has burst the bubbles of pleasure and profit, materialism and laughter. The sharpness of death pierces all our pretensions of ultimate happiness. But now the Teacher does a surprising thing. He bursts death's bubble.

The Teacher's prescription for living the good life doesn't seem like much: 'A person can do nothing better than to eat and drink and find satisfaction in their toil' (2:24). At first glance this seems like the nihilistic creed: 'Eat, drink and be merry, for tomorrow we die.' In fact, we are going to see several differences between this slogan and the world-view of Ecclesiastes, and here's the first one. Some say 'eat, drink and be merry' because that's *all* there is; the Teacher says 'eat, drink and be merry' because that's *what* there is. God has given the good things of this world to us and they are their own reward.

When we accept in a deep way that we are going to die, that reality can stop us expecting too much from all the good things we pursue. We learn to pursue them for what they are in themselves, rather than what we need them to be to make us happy. Death reorients us to our limitations as creatures and helps us to see God's good gifts right in front of us all the time each and every day of our lives. Instead of using these gifts as means to a greater end of securing ultimate gain in the world, we take the time to live inside the gifts themselves and see the hand of God in them. Ordinarily, we eat and drink simply as fuel to enable us to keep going with our work. Ordinarily, we work not just to earn a living, but to find satisfaction and purpose and very likely to make a reputation for ourselves and to achieve success. What if the pleasure of food is a daily joy that we ungratefully overlook? What if our work was never intended to make us successful, but simply to make us faithful and generous? What if it is death which shows us that this is how we are meant to live?

We saw in chapter 1 that at the heart of our human condition is an unwillingness to accept things as they really are. We long for lives of permanence in a world of constant change and we strive to achieve it. We long for change in a world of permanent repetition and we dream of how to interrupt it. The same idea is present in this section of Ecclesiastes, for one of the striking features of the vast projects undertaken in 2:4–9 is how the language evokes the Garden of Eden, as if the Teacher were trying to recreate God's good and perfect world. But it cannot be done. The world in which we live is now fallen and cursed – God has placed a fracture in the fabric of the universe, and things are now not what they should be (1:15).

We are limited because we are creatures, and because we are fallen creatures, we now have in-built flawed assumptions about what it means to live in the world. We tend to use the world around us – work, possessions, people – as leverage for our own purposes to achieve our own goals. They are the tools we use to master life for our own ends. But the Teacher's whole point in this section is to show us that the world cannot be leveraged to suit me, and life is meant to be enjoyed not mastered. Here is how Jeffrey Meyers puts it:

> Realising this can help you deal with life in a way that honours God. For example, do not be surprised to find yourself in a frustrating situation from which you cannot escape by means of controlling it. Not everything can be fixed! Not everything is a problem to be solved. Some things must be borne, must be suffered and endured. Wisdom does not teach us how to master the world. It does not give us techniques for programming life such that life becomes orderly and predictable.[11]

It is interesting that from 1:14 to 2:23 God has been entirely absent from the writer's frame of reference; the striving self is at the centre. But now in 2:24–26 God is mentioned three times in quick succession. The emphasis is on what God *gives*. He is the one who gives enjoyment and satisfaction in life: 'This too, I see, is from the hand of God' (2:24). It's a very profound and beautiful point and one we know is true. Endless enjoyment does not come in the box with your iPhone – if it did, why have you been considering that upgrade? Enjoyment is not automatically part of sex. It is not on the keyring to your dream house. It doesn't ride with you on the passenger seat in your new car. We all know what it is like to have tasted the best life has to offer and still to be left wondering what comes next.

The Teacher tells us that God has to give us enjoyment, or the thing itself (phone, sex, house, car) will leave us unsatisfied. And the way God gives us enjoyment in his gifts is by giving us perspective on ourselves. When we know that the gift is not meant to be a stepping stone to greater things, when we realize we are not meant to rule the world, or master our destiny, or achieve ultimate gain through our careers, then we discover that enjoyment or joy is 'itself the reward that we may expect from life and all our effort expended in living it . . . There is no surplus to joy beyond joy itself. There is indeed no pathway to joy except by refusing to pursue it and to grasp at it.'[12]

God is also the one who 'gives wisdom, knowledge and happiness' (2:26). It is so striking that now, at the end of the Teacher's epic quest through life for happiness, he discovers where it comes from. Not from his striving, but from God's giving. God gives these things to the person 'who pleases him'.

This is just the first ray of light, and at this point in the book it may not seem to shine very brightly. It may seem rather abstract and out of reach somehow. But stick with it. Although we are only just beginning to see this in Ecclesiastes, the Teacher is deeply committed to a way of being in the world that locates us in a right relationship to God and a right relationship to our neighbour.

From these two things flow all the happiness in life we will ever need, for it is there we see ourselves as we truly are: dependent creatures made for relationship with our Creator.

Questions for discussion or personal reflection
1. What is your motivation for getting up each morning?
2. What do the lives of people you know reveal about what they think will make them happy?
3. How would you describe 'true joy' to a friend who knew nothing of this?
4. What strategies do you think people you know, including yourself, use to avoid facing the reality of death?
5. What do you make of the idea that death can give us the perspective we need to begin to enjoy life?

3

Doing time

'All shall be well, and all manner of things shall be well.'
  Julian of Norwich, *Revelations of Divine Love*

There is a time for everything,
and a season for every activity under the heavens:

> a time to be born and a time to die,
> a time to plant and a time to uproot,
> a time to kill and a time to heal,
> a time to tear down and a time to build,
> a time to weep and a time to laugh,
> a time to mourn and a time to dance,
> a time to scatter stones and a time to gather them,
> a time to embrace and a time to refrain from embracing,
> a time to search and a time to give up,
> a time to keep and a time to throw away,
> a time to tear and a time to mend,
> a time to be silent and a time to speak,
> a time to love and a time to hate,
> a time for war and a time for peace.

What do workers gain from their toil? I have seen the burden God has laid on the human race. He has made everything beautiful in its time. He has also set eternity in the human heart; yet no one can fathom what God has done from beginning to end. I know that there is nothing better for people than to be happy and to do good while they live. That each of them may eat and drink, and find satisfaction in all their toil – this is the gift of God. I know that everything God does will endure for ever; nothing can be added to it and nothing taken from it. God does it so that people will fear him.

> Whatever is has already been,
>> and what will be has been before;
>> and God will call the past to account.

And I saw something else under the sun:

> In the place of judgment – wickedness was there,
>> in the place of justice – wickedness was there.

I said to myself,

> 'God will bring into judgment
>> both the righteous and the wicked,
> for there will be a time for every activity,
>> a time to judge every deed.'

I also said to myself, 'As for humans, God tests them so that they may see that they are like the animals. Surely the fate of human beings is like that of the animals; the same fate awaits them both: as one dies, so dies the other. All have the same breath; humans have no advantage over animals. Everything is meaningless. All go to the same place; all come from dust, and to dust all return.

Who knows if the human spirit rises upward and if the spirit of the animal goes down into the earth?'

So I saw that there is nothing better for a person than to enjoy their work, because that is their lot. For who can bring them to see what will happen after them?

(Ecclesiastes 3:1–22)

Everything in its place

I recently built the Millennium Falcon.

For those who don't know, the Falcon is one of the greatest spaceships a galaxy far, far away has ever seen. Flown by Han Solo and his sidekick Chewbacca in *Star Wars*, it is capable of entering hyperdrive at just the right time, and while it might look like a beaten-up old wreck, everyone knows that's part of its enduring charm. And I helped to build it.

The Lego version, that is.

My children and I opened the beautiful box at the start of a glorious holiday in south Devon, poured over the 1,254 pieces of the famous craft, and my eldest son set about piecing it together. It took him a total of nine hours. Patiently, lovingly, brick by brick, section by section, and with growing excitement, he saw the work of his hands create something spectacular. Even his mother agreed it was superb, and she couldn't tell the Millennium Falcon from the Starship Enterprise.

If you have ever built anything by Lego – or from IKEA – you will know that success is achieved when you work piece by piece, using each one in all the right places in all the right ways and at all the right times. If you're trying to build a model to match the picture on the box, then going freestyle is usually a recipe for disaster.

As I watched my son work, it occurred to me how life is like a construction exercise. Our lives are made up of so many different pieces – people, events, circumstances, times, places – which are all being locked together to make our individual stories. Sometimes we don't see the significance of a tiny piece of the story until later on. Often there seems to be a brick missing and it's hard to keep going without it. Or there's tremendous joy and satisfaction as a particular piece clicks into place and crowns a part of our life project.

The difference between real life and Lego construction, however, is that we are not the ones with the instruction blueprint laid out in front of us. God is. We have individual pieces in our hands, and in the Bible God has given us enough explanation to set us building, but only he has the master plan. We are building our lives and we have an idea of how we want to do it, and how we hope it will turn out, but there is so much about what shape our lives will take that we cannot control.

The essence of Ecclesiastes 3

In chapter 1 of Ecclesiastes the Teacher introduced his main thesis: death puts an end to our repetitive quest for greatness and gain, and instead teaches us that we are simply part of the generation who came after the last one and before the next. But it's not just that the whole of our lives comes and goes like a vapour. In chapter 2 the Teacher explained that all the pursuits and pleasures we give ourselves to within our lives also slip through our fingers with little lasting satisfaction.

Now in chapter 3 the Teacher brings together both the big picture (the whole of life) and the individual parts (the seasons of life) and begins to explain why our lack of control over either is the very thing that can give us hope. There are many ways to embrace our frailty, and nearly all of them involve thinking clearly about time. It is part of living well to accept two things: first, we are enclosed within time's bounds, and second, God is not. What we do comes and goes, but 'everything God does will endure for ever' (3:14). We are each building the project of 'me', constructing the edifice of our lives, but as we do so, we are neither architect nor site manager. We are each writing the story of our lives, but we are not the main Author.

Ecclesiastes 3 is a very beautiful chapter, with famous words of poetry often read at funerals, even humanist ones. As we will see, however, the beauty of the Teacher's poetry in verses 1–8 is only half the story; we need the punch of his prose in verses 9–22 if we are actually to find any joy and hope in the poetry.

1 The powerful pattern of his poetry (verses 1–8)
Just as the created world has a rhythmic pattern built into it, so too our lives within this world experience their own regularities and cadences which ebb and flow with the rolling years. Ecclesiastes 3 gives us a poem to show this.

The statement in verse 1 – there is a time and a season for everything – is fleshed out in verses 2–8 with an artful literary technique which places polar opposites or extreme positions side by side, 'as a way of embracing everything that lies between them (e.g. north and south, heaven and earth)'.[1] So with 'a time to be born and a time to die' (verse 2), the whole of life is captured as being something which has a time for its beginning, a time for its end, and a time for everything else that happens between the decisive moments of start and finish.

After stating the big picture of life and death, the rest of the verses move through different experiences of life and all the varied human activities which most of us engage in or encounter at one time or another. There does not seem to be a logical progression or natural connection between one set of extremes and those that come after or before. If there is any structure, it most likely lies in the fact that the list of opposites is made up of twenty-eight items in fourteen pairs; this means the list is comprised of multiples of seven, the number which symbolizes perfection in the Bible.[2] It is a skilful way of again emphasizing the totality of things that are contained within any human life. This is a complete summary of the seasons of life.

It is a mistake to extract these verses from the whole chapter (as is often done) and think they can have their real meaning displayed without looking at how the Teacher follows them in verses 9–22. The poetry is setting up a problem which the prose will seek to resolve. At the same time, however, there is a wonderful richness to the poetry that is worth lingering over.

To begin with, note how the poem expresses the beautiful complexity of life. Some of the opposites in the list can be grouped together into a basic pattern of bad times and good times: there is a time for killing and a time for healing, a time to love and a time to hate, a time for war and a time for peace. But not all seasons have an opposite which is either straightforwardly good or bad: there is a time to embrace and a time to refrain; there is a time to be silent and a time to speak. Each of these can be good when done at the right time in the right way. Others seem even more ambiguous to us: there is a time to search and a time to give up. Which one of these is favourable or unfavourable? Again, as with chapter 1, the form of the poem is part of the meaning of its content: life is complex, full of good times, hard times, in-between times, and a whole manner of lifestyle choices and decisions which often require a wisdom that seems to escape us. There is a time for every single one of these things.

Observe as well how the combined effect of the poem puts flesh on the skeleton of a human life. There are seasons in the world which act upon us (war and peace), but almost every pair in the poem involves our connectedness to others between the moments of our birth and death. We are profoundly relational beings, and most of the seasons of our lives are taken up with navigating the different stages of our relationships and the effects they have on us. We dance at a wedding, and we mourn the loss of the one we danced with. We laugh together, and we weep for what the people we used to laugh with have done to us. Without thinking, we reach out and touch, but we instinctively respect a different emotional and physical boundary with someone else. We grow to love some people, and come to hate others.

If we were somehow to take the seasons of life out of the web of relationships in which we are enmeshed, our lives would become flat and monotonous. We check our calendars every day, but we don't set the seasons of life just by the patterns of the sun and the moon. Rather, our times are marked by being a daughter and a sister, becoming a wife and a lover, then a mother and a grandmother, and a widow. These are the seasons God gives. The times he grants are bound to the presence or absence of relationship.[3]

The Teacher is seeking to give us perspective on each of the items in his patterned opposites, while pointing us to the perplexity of this rhythmically ordered arrangement of time. Life is full of flaws. Killing, tearing down, weeping, mourning, hating, warring: these are the times of life we will experience which show us in the most painful of ways that we live east of Eden and under the curse. More than this, the fact that there is no chronological sequence or discernible purpose to the order of each of these items is itself part of the Teacher's point that we have no control over any of these things. We make real, responsible decisions every single day, but in reality we each know that the seasons of life are almost completely out of our hands. There is a time for everything, but we are not arranging them on our stopwatch. 'Three hours for mirth today and next week I will have just twenty minutes of sorrow, please. Following that I will embark on an entirely new chapter of life with great success and in two and a half years I will be happy to move on to something new.' We all know life is not like this. So what can we do about it?

Each of the individual aspects of the curse displayed in this poetry combine to point to one great flaw – and here is where I want to make good on my claim that this beautiful poetry on its own can actually do us more harm than good. For notice how the Teacher follows the poetry immediately in verse 9: 'What do workers gain from their toil?' This is the most powerful of sucker punches.

There is a time for everything, life is a lyrical arrangement of good and bad, of relational complexity and nuanced subtleties, and at the end of it all you go in a box in the cold, hard ground. What have you gained after living all the seasons of life? Nothing. You're dead. You experienced it all, you came and went, and look: you have no lasting gain. It is vital to see that there is nothing in the first eight verses of chapter 3 that could not have been written by an atheist philosopher or the Poet Laureate. Anyone with enough experience can dramatize life in this way, and sum it all up with a lilting flow of rhythmical patterns.

It's why I've heard these words at a humanist funeral, but I have yet to hear a celebrant advance to verse 9. Is it possible that it doesn't much matter whether you read verses 1–8 out at a humanist funeral or a Christian one? For it is still a funeral. Joe Bloggs might have led a varied life in all its richness, but what has he gained now? Nothing. He's dead. It's over.

As we've already seen, one of the questions we have to ask when reading Ecclesiastes is what separates its message from the epithet of nihilism: 'Eat, drink and be merry, for tomorrow we die.' Ecclesiastes may sound very similar in places (remember 2:24), but in fact it is miles away from this kind of world-view.

It is the prose section of chapter 3 that begins to show us why.

2 The comforting challenge of his prose (verses 9–22)

It is meant to be a great shock that the poetry of verses 1–8 is followed by the harsh reality of verse 9. The patterned order in the world does not lead us to find gain in the midst of it all. The rhythms rumble through our life, we find them happening to us often without our awareness of what is really going on, and the very fact that life keeps changing leaves us with no lasting success or feeling of deep satisfaction.

But now the Teacher adds a wonderful perspective, and it's one that we're meant to have with us as we read the rest of his book: the times of my life are not the only times there are. There is a time to be born and a time to die, and there is a time for judgment. One of the ways we learn to live by preparing to die is by realizing that death means judgment, and that this is a good thing. It gives my present actions meaning and weight, and it gives my experienced losses and injustices a voice in God's presence. What is past may be past, but what is past is not forgotten to God, and because he is in charge and lives for ever, one day all will be well. Every single thing that happens will have its day in court.

This brings both comfort and challenge. Let's think about each of these.

Comfort
Plenty of my children's frustrations are because my wife and I see a bigger picture than they do, and we are often working towards goals they cannot really understand. What to eat,

what to wear, when to go to bed, where they're allowed to go and not allowed to go – their little lives find their rhythms and patterns within the ordered whole that we their parents seek to provide. Although they don't always recognize it, this is meant to provide them with tremendous security and the right and best kind of freedom. They are free from the stress and worry of trying to co-ordinate events and tie up loose ends and balance decisions about time and place, and how to get one of them to swimming and another to gymnastics while preparing the dinner and remembering to cut the grass and get to the prayer meeting on time.

All grown-ups are like children when it comes to our own lives and God's ordering of them. We have the rhythmical pattern of the things that fill our lives, but God does not exist within the same timetable. What he does 'will endure for ever' (verse 14), and he is the one who sees the end from the beginning and so is able to make 'everything beautiful in its time' (verse 11). In other words, because God lives for ever and I will not, I can experience the several different times of my life knowing that they are part of a bigger picture which I cannot see, but which is visible to a good and wise God who sees the whole as beautiful.

Part of being wise in this world is learning to accept that we have only very limited access to the big picture. To be sure, we often *want* access to it – for God has 'set eternity in the human heart' – but the point is that we 'cannot fathom what God has done from beginning to end' (3:11). God is not being unkind to us by not sharing it; the point is that we are not built to understand the big picture precisely because we live in time and God does not. If we could see the end from the beginning, and understand how a billion lives and a thousand generations and unspeakable sorrows and untold joys are all woven into a tapestry of perfect beauty, then we would be God.

This means that part of growing up in the world is learning to grow small. God intends us to be like children who trust their parents to know best because they can see what the children can't see and they know what the children are not yet able to know. And here's the thing – the relationship of trust is built on the character of the parents. If the parents are good and wise and kind, then the child who cannot see the end from the beginning has nothing to fear.

The Teacher makes it crystal clear to us that we have a wonderful reason for trusting a timeless God with the times of our lives: he is perfectly just. In verse 15 the phrase 'God will call the past to account' is literally: 'God will seek what has been chased away.' This imagery is suggestive of shepherding, where a farmer deliberately seeks out the animal that has fled the fold and goes to find it and bring it back. In this case it is all the events of human history that time has chased away into the past, and to us they are gone and lost for ever. But not to God. He will dial back time and fetch the past into his present to bring it to account.

We are endlessly fascinated with time travel. Whether it's the cult classic *Back to the Future*, or the powerful and moving *Interstellar*, there is a reason why time travel features so often on the big screen. There is something mind-boggling about being present to ourselves in our past, or entering the world our ancestors were part of while belonging in the future they never saw. It makes for brilliant entertainment because it's such an escape from reality. But Ecclesiastes makes the even more astonishing claim that living well here and now in this world depends on time travel being possible. Not to us, but to God.

I look at pictures of my children when they were three years younger than they are now and I cannot even remember that they looked like that. The photographs have frozen a moment in time, and with their aid I am transported back to that day on the beach, or in the park, or round the Christmas tree, but the moment is gone and I cannot get it back. But the Teacher is saying that God is not bound by time in the way that I am. And while I might feel sentimental or nostalgic for the happy family snap, they are not really moments in time that I need to get back.

I do have plenty of other moments in the past, however, that I am very glad God will one day call back and seek out. In my finite story I am often left grasping after several different threads and cannot seem to weave them into one coherent whole. My story has broken characters, jarring interruptions, unexpected joys, relationships caught up in unresolved tensions and difficulties. My life story has unexplained contradictions, I have plenty of unanswered questions and, in God's kindness and mercy, I have as yet unfinished chapters. But my story is not *the* story. '*The* story reveals that there will be a time of judgment, and believers trust that judgment will finally prevail.'[4]

Do you see the beauty of this? One of the things that causes greatest pain in our world is what the Teacher sees in verse 16:

> In the place of judgment – wickedness was there,
> in the place of justice – wickedness was there.

Craig Bartholomew observes that *time* and *place* are the two great co-ordinates of created life, and when our law courts are not the place where justice finds its appropriate time, the very order of creation itself breaks down.[5]

Our longing for justice is hard-wired. Deny a bereaved parent justice for their child's killer, and there are no words for the terror and fury that can consume a human heart and overwhelm a broken home. Trample on someone's rights and dignity and demean their self-worth and get off scot-free for having done so, and we give birth to the kind of indignation that can smoulder for decades with devastating effect. The world is not meant to be like this. Will there ever be a time for justice?

The answer is yes. God will retrieve every single injustice, and every single time and every single activity. Every single deed that has ever broken his holy law and tarnished his beautiful world and damaged his image-bearers – every one of those moments will be answerable to God. Every tear and every sighing sorrow for my wrongs, whether through things I have done or had done to me – each one will be sought out by the God who is perfect justice, truth, mercy and love.

Challenge
This should affect my life in another way too. Knowing that God is outside of time and sees it all and will, in the end, bring to judgment both the righteous and the wicked, stops me needing to be in control of everything that happens to me. The message of Ecclesiastes is not that life is full of good times and bad times and so you just have to roll with the punches. Rather, the message is that life is full of good times and bad times which we cannot control, but the patterning of our lives in this way is part of a bigger pattern which God controls. It's not just that good follows bad, follows good again, and that's the end of it. The point is that I can live within this rhythmic pattern and accept not having all the answers to my times of pain yet. *Yet*. This is the key. Every time of mine will have its day in court. So while I wait, how then should I live?

Zack Eswine says that 'time, in God's hands, graciously apprentices us'.[6] To be forewarned is to be forearmed. With eyes to see, we are meant to learn that where we are now is not where we will always be. When we are dancing, most of us do not realize we are creating memories with people whom we will one day mourn. When we are weeping, we rarely think that in a few weeks' time we could be laughing again. Maybe we have known only peace and never war. Perhaps it is hard to imagine a day when to touch will be less wise than to refrain, or that conversations lie ahead of us which one day we would give anything to erase because we foolishly chose speech over silence. Nearly always we live only in and for each moment. What difference would it make to our now to begin to live in the light of the fact that there will be a then?

Ecclesiastes tells us to learn now, today, that there really is a time for everything. Learning now that the season or seasons I am in will not always be the season of my life can at least help to prepare me for the chapters of my life God has yet to write. It does not mean that giving up or throwing away is going to be any easier when they come, but it may help me not to be taken by surprise. As Eswine says, 'Many of our frustrations rise from our blindness to the change of season or to the pain or joy of them, and we struggle to adjust our expectations.'[7] It is possible that actively embracing the fact of change in advance of change can help us to adjust our step that little bit more readily when autumn or winter is upon us.

Living like this is also what helps us to realize that so much of the time we use our times to seek satisfaction, rather than living in the times God has given and so receiving satisfaction from him as a gift. Satisfaction comes when you know you are a time-bound creature and God is the eternal Creator. Satisfaction lodges in my heart when I accept the boundaries of my creaturely existence and accept the seasons of my life as coming from his good and wise hands. Accepting these things is the gift of God, for, left to our own devices, we accept neither. I often refuse to accept that I am a creature by never expecting to walk through deep valleys but only experience the mountain tops. Am I in a season of sorrow and despair? I often refuse to accept that this has come to me from his fatherly care. It is easy to stop believing that God will bring every single one of my moments into his eternal present and put right what has gone wrong.

When my son set about building the Millennium Falcon, he was a mini-god with a mini-creation. He had the plan and he knew what he was doing. He knew where everything was meant to go, in which order, and at what time. He knew what the finished product would look like. But what I didn't tell you at the start of the chapter is that along the way the construction process saw a few tears. There were frustrations at the instructions, and impatience with my interventions. Some pieces somehow went missing. The finished product looks magnificent, but to those in the know, it is not perfect.

Living well in God's world means recognizing that when it comes to our own lives, we are not mini-gods, and this is his creation, not ours. We have all the pieces of our life given to us, and things come and go and seasons change, and it is only God who knows exactly where everything is meant to go, in which order, at what time and why.

Questions for discussion or personal reflection

1. What things do you seek to control? What might it look like to surrender control?
2. How could you have a wiser perspective on your time?
3. What might it look like to 'grow small' (see p. 46)?
4. How can we help one another to 'embrace the fact of change in advance' (see p. 49)?
5. 'There is a time for judgment' (p. 48). What difference could that truth make to the worries you have at the moment?

4

Living a life less upwardly mobile

> *'When a man comes to die, no matter what his talents and influence and genius, if he dies unloved his life must be a failure to him and his dying a cold horror.'*
> John Steinbeck, *East of Eden*

Again I looked and saw all the oppression that was taking place under the sun:

I saw the tears of the oppressed –
   and they have no comforter;
power was on the side of their oppressors –
   and they have no comforter.
And I declared that the dead,
   who had already died,
are happier than the living,
   who are still alive.
But better than both
   is the one who has never been born,
who has not seen the evil
   that is done under the sun.

And I saw that all toil and all achievement spring from one person's envy of another. This too is meaningless, a chasing after the wind.

Fools fold their hands
    and ruin themselves.
Better one handful with tranquillity
    than two handfuls with toil
    and chasing after the wind.

Again I saw something meaningless under the sun:

there was a man all alone;
    he had neither son nor brother.
There was no end to his toil,
    yet his eyes were not content with his wealth.
'For whom am I toiling,' he asked,
    'and why am I depriving myself of enjoyment?'
This too is meaningless –
    a miserable business!
Two are better than one,
    because they have a good return for their labour:
if either of them falls down,
    one can help the other up.
But pity anyone who falls
    and has no one to help them up.
Also, if two lie down together, they will keep warm.
    But how can one keep warm alone?
Though one may be overpowered,
    two can defend themselves.
A cord of three strands is not quickly broken.

Better a poor but wise youth than an old but foolish king who no longer knows how to heed a warning. The youth may have come from prison to the kingship, or he may have been born in poverty within his kingdom. I saw that all who lived and walked under the sun followed the youth, the king's successor. There was no end to all the people who were before them. But those who came later were not pleased with the successor. This too is meaningless, a chasing after the wind.

(Ecclesiastes 4:1-16)

Where am I going with my life?

This is the dominant question of the modern mind, and it is a question that we are trying to answer all the time. Some of us spend a great deal of time explicitly pondering it. Others might say it's not really a question we've ever found particularly troubling. But each of us lives inside that question, and in a hundred different ways we have already spent a lot of time today answering it for ourselves. If somehow there was to be a digital recorder inside our brain that replayed our private thought world on to a big screen, I wager we would be amazed to realize just how much of our thinking is taken up with one little two-letter word: *me*.

The big issue of 'where am I going with my life?' tends to be micro-managed inside our heads. Usually it's simply: 'How am I doing today?' We go through the day with a sense of whether we are happy or sad, or under pressure and stressed and tired, or relaxed and carefree. Or maybe none of the above at all – we are simply busy and focused on the task in hand. At work, at home, in relationships with others, we are always processing the world through our own eyes, responding to what our circumstances are doing to us and how they make us feel. Sometimes in the midst of all this day-to-day existing, we are taken up with bigger issues: why am I working so hard – is it worth it? What am I living for? What am I achieving, or failing to achieve? But my point is simply this: whether in trivial or important ways, the one person I am *always* acutely aware of is me.

There is an old saying that you are not what you think you are; but what you think, you are. So just stop and reflect: whom do you spend most of your time thinking about?

The preacher in Ecclesiastes takes it for granted that it's you. Every person fills their thoughts and plans with themselves, as they constantly work out how to navigate the world in a way that will give meaning and happiness.

And, says the Teacher, that is the very source of our pain.

In this chapter, I want to show you that Ecclesiastes gives us a new question to ask. The Teacher offers a whole new way of living. He longs to see it absorbed into our bloodstream so that we experience a radical change in the orientation of our hearts and the way we see the world. He gives us a question to free us from ourselves: how are *we* doing? We, not I. That's the chapter in a nutshell. We, not me.

If you can live in this world in such a way that the person or people beside you – your friend, your spouse, your children, your brother, your sister, the people God has put in your path – are your waking concern and your dominant focus, then you will find happiness. If your head hits the pillow at night full of questions about how you might help and serve someone else, and how you can be a certain kind of person for them, then you will find a gladness and contentment that nothing else can match.

As we begin, I want you to notice what the Teacher is *not* saying. You might expect him to say that if you live for others, then you'll be more spiritual. Or more godly. You'll be a growing Christian. It is certainly true that you will be all those things, but that is not the aspect of life which the Teacher is painting in this part of his book. You will be happier. The word he uses is 'tranquillity' (verse 6). It simply means rest – peace of mind and calmness of soul. It's a word to capture the deep well-being of the person who knows their place in the world, content with the boundary lines of their life and able to enjoy the fruits of their labours with a cheerful heart. The way to arrive in that place of rest is to live for we, not me.

The Teacher is adding more colour and detail to his developing portrait of the wise and faithful life lived under the sun. So far, he has highlighted the innate human desire to get ahead of creation itself, rather than living in harmony with the restraints both the world and time naturally impose on us. Now in chapter 4 he highlights the innate desire to get ahead of my neighbour rather than living gladly with the responsibilities which he or she places on me.

So the picture is beginning to look like this: neither the world nor your own life is completely within your control. If you spend your whole life refusing to accept that the day of your death is approaching, if you live and work 24/7 thinking that by doing so you can get ahead of the game and have a better life by making money, or that you can understand the world by getting the right degrees or reading the right books, or if you think you can really leave a lasting mark on the world through what you do, then you are spending your life trying to punch above your weight. We are creatures, not the Creator, and the Teacher is out to shatter my illusion that I can be like God. I want to have it all, know it all and be remembered by all for all time. No, says the Teacher, life is gift, not gain.

The universe we inhabit and the life you have today come from God's hand as something you do not deserve. Your life is on loan for a short while, and one day God will call time and take it back, just like the library will recall that overdue book on your shelf. So embrace life for what it is, rather than what you'd like it to be. Live it before God with reverence and obedience. For this is the pathway to joy, even though as you walk it, there will be mystery and pain. Have some nice food.

Enjoy a good wine if you want – but be sure to *enjoy* whatever good things come your way.

Chapter 4 adds a new layer to this picture. As you enjoy, share. Share what you have with others. It's as simple as that.

In fact, this is intimately connected to what it means to really know God. Jesus said the most important commandment is this:

> 'Hear, O Israel: the Lord our God, the Lord is one. Love the Lord your God with all your heart and with all your soul and with all your mind and with all your strength.' The second is this: 'Love your neighbour as yourself.' There is no commandment greater than these.
>
> (Mark 12:29–31)

We are going to look at Ecclesiastes 4 through this whole-Bible lens. The Teacher tells us that we have to share what we enjoy because there are two ways to live in the world. You can either hate your neighbour and so destroy yourself (4:1–6), or you can love your neighbour and so love yourself (4:7–16).

1 Hating my neighbour, destroying myself

In every age and in every part, the world is full to the brim with love of self and hatred of others. Up to this point in Ecclesiastes, the Teacher has spoken about 'wickedness', evil described in general terms. But now he focuses his lens and zooms in on a particular kind of evil: 'I looked and saw all the *oppression* that was taking place under the sun' (4:1, italics mine).

He is confronted by outrageous violence in every area of the globe. He could see the tears of the victims, but there was no one to wipe them away. He saw the iron rod of the dictator crushing the weak, and there was no one to protect the innocent and shield the vulnerable. As he looked, it became unbearable to keep on looking, so much so that he congratulates the dead on being dead for they are spared the misery he sees. And never being born at all is better than being dead after having been alive. The happiest state of all is not even to exist in the first place.

Does this sound too bleak for you? Can someone who believes in God utter words like these? Some writers do want to suggest, of course, that this is not the Teacher's own perspective and that he is simply describing life without God. But that is far too simplistic. As believers, we have to come to terms honestly with the world as it really is, and the Teacher is looking at the world as it really is.

So in these verses the Teacher simply describes how it feels to keep watching the news report about 'Baby P' instead of flicking the channels because you can't bear it. Peter Connelly (referred to as 'Baby P' during the trial of his parents) was a seventeen-month-old boy in London who died after suffering over fifty injuries during an eight-month period. During that time he was repeatedly seen by healthcare professionals, who failed to notice the harm he was enduring. He was left in a home of unspeakable abuse and trauma by people who had the power to rescue him.

A paramedic friend of mine was called to assist a man who had fallen at home. In a filthy living room with a foul stench, he and his colleague discovered a sixty-year-old man who had been left to lie in the same spot for over two weeks by his son. When they tried to move him, his skin came away from his clothes and body. He had to be wrapped in burn dressings after lying in his own urine for so long. In Birmingham, a toddler called Kristiana Logina died of septic shock after her mother held her under a scalding shower as a form of punishment. She lived with her injuries for two weeks, and eventually died because her parents had refused to seek medical help for her wounds.

Allowing yourself to dwell on such atrocities becomes unbearable. The death of defenceless children is one of the worst evils in our world. It is one of the most upsetting scenes to witness and the most crushing of losses to endure. The smallest coffins are the heaviest.

As believers, we must never be trite and simplistic when relating the good news of Christ to a world of pain. In Mark 7:31–37 Jesus heals a man who was deaf and could hardly speak, but he does not do so unmoved by the man's brokenness and suffering: '[Jesus] looked up to heaven and with a deep sigh said to him, *"Ephphatha!"* (which means "Be opened!").' Elsewhere, Jesus sighs like this on encountering the hard-hearted unbelief of the Pharisees (Mark 8:12). The Greek word used for 'sigh' is *anastenazo*, the same one used by the apostle Paul in Romans 8:22, where creation 'groans' under the trauma of the curse God has placed on it. When the Lord Jesus came face to face with his good world twisted out of shape – whether outwardly in damaged body or inwardly in calloused heart – he groaned at the curse. This is why the apostle Paul can call Jesus our wisdom (1 Corinthians 1:24). His response to his broken creation is the same as that of the Teacher in Ecclesiastes.

It is gloriously true that Jesus Christ is the one whose life, death and resurrection have begun to remake the world. He does this in spectacular ways. In Mark 7:37 the people respond to Christ's healing of the deaf and dumb man by saying, 'He has done everything well', words that echo the creation story where God saw all that he had made and 'it was very good'. In each individual miracle performed by Christ, the new creation arrived. With each restored limb and revitalized body, the kingdom of God on earth, life as it was meant to be, had broken in.[1] But here is what we must remember: for now it is partial. It is not complete – yet.

Ecclesiastes knows how we will feel if we stare long enough and hard enough at the way the world really is. We are simply not used to doing this. We cope with it through distraction. We have *Comic Relief*, so that we can stop the images of hunger and poverty and deprivation being relentless and unbearable. Would we really be able to cope with it if the terrible images weren't followed by light-hearted diversion? We pay money for laughter so that we can help the suffering but not have to look at it for too long. But if there really wasn't anywhere to avert our eyes, maybe we would find ourselves thinking it's a blessing to have no idea what evil is in the first place. Perhaps we would count the unborn among the most fortunate people in the world.

Sometimes there are no answers. You cannot always give help to the person who comes to see you in floods of tears. You can't fix everything. And when we look at the broken, fallen world through a biblical lens, what we see is that the world is a place where my neighbour can be damned so long as I can be king. It's a place where we often relentlessly pursue the neighbour above us by willingly stepping on the head of the neighbour beneath us. When we pursue gain because we think that's all there is to be had, others are going to get hurt. That's what happens.

Believers can never afford to fold their arms and say, 'Well, that's just the way it is. Tough.' That is as far from genuine Christian faith as it is possible to get. There is something unique, however, about the Christian approach to injustice and oppression. Any relief organization will be eloquent in their explanation of the damage that the powerful can inflict on the weak. But the Bible is just as concerned with the damage done to the *oppressor* in their acts of oppression.

Verse 4 contains an incredible observation: 'I saw that all toil and all achievement spring from one person's envy of another.' Envy has long been considered one of the seven deadly sins and for a very good reason. It is so subtle. Consider the old saying: any friend can share your sorrows and failures, but it takes a true friend to share your joys and successes. That is exactly right. When we see a friend succeed and make things work, we smile and pat her on the back, but deep down we envy her because she has made us feel worse about ourselves. When our friend falls flat on his face, our sinfulness is such that we can watch him mess up, and even as we hug him, his failure makes us feel so much better about ourselves.

Deep in our hearts we want to be noticed and to be the focus of attention, and that desire is capable of driving all we do and the reason we do it. Jesus says I am to love you. But what I often feel is: what will it take to get what you have? If I envy you through loving you (because I love you only to get something from you), then not only am I engaged in oppressing you; I have a cancer that eats at my heart and can destroy me even as I destroy you. This is because I have dressed up my selfishness in generosity and deceived both of us in the process.

Rebecca Konyndyk DeYoung recounts the poem of Victor Hugo in which Envy and Greed are each granted the opportunity to receive whatever they wish, on the condition that the other receives a double portion. Envy says, 'I wish to be blind in one eye.' Konyndyk DeYoung explains, 'The envious person resents another person's good gifts because they are superior to his or her own. It's not just that the other person is better; it is that by comparison their superiority makes you feel your own lack, your own inferiority, more acutely.'[2] So dragging other people down and taking from them what they have can make us feel better about ourselves.

The Teacher is probing deep inside the human heart. All this striving and toiling, working and working and working: it is all motivated by me. But what about others? What do they need? How can I be a giver instead of a getter, a servant of others instead of lord of myself? When we stop and think about serving and loving our neighbour, it prevents two extremes: idle laziness (verse 5) and manic busyness (verse 6).

Laziness is a way of hating your neighbour. You have nothing to give them. 'Fools fold their hands and ruin themselves' is more literally: 'The fool embraces his hands and devours his own flesh.' The Teacher makes a deliberately extreme statement to illustrate the corrosive effects of inverted excess. Instead of embracing life and giving himself to others, the sluggard gives himself to himself, so that in the end all that he has left is himself – and that won't last for long. There is no food in the cupboard, and he has to eat himself to survive. Now you've never seen a lazy person actually eat himself, but you might have seen a lazy person erode their self-control and capacity for care, and in the end erase even their self-respect. They ruin themselves. Workaholics are often warned that on their deathbed they will not wish they had spent more time at the office. Ecclesiastes warns us that certain people on their deathbed will wish they had spent at least some time at the office.

No better than this is the opposite extreme of frantic busyness. You know the kind of person – feverishly running from one thing to the next, and all the while trying to mask a dissatisfaction with life because they're always working for tomorrow. We usually think life tomorrow is going to be better than life today, because tomorrow we'll have achieved something new: tomorrow we'll spend more time with the Bible, we'll finally tidy the house; tomorrow we'll complete the dream move, the promotion, the degree, a marriage, the deadline. The Teacher's point is that to live this way is like shooting yourself in one foot so that you can hop more quickly with the other. Why not stop and enjoy today in very real ways? Tomorrow's promotion will bring more pressure. The higher degree will just teach you how little you know. The marriage will connect you to another sinner for life. The deadline will pass only for another to come racing towards you.

Manic busyness is endemic in Christian ministry, for it is a bottomless pit of good and godly gospel tasks to be accomplished. There's always more to do and perennial guilt to live with when it is not being done. Yet some of it, too, is a chasing after the wind, because we try to gain the kind of things in ministry that we were never called to receive.

Michael Horton reminds pastors that they are not here to leave a legacy by their ministry. We have no legacy. Christ has the legacy – the covenant – which he put into effect by his death and which he now dispenses from heaven by his Word and Spirit. Pastors need to realize that they 'come and go, but the legacy keeps on being dispersed'.[3] In his memoir, *The Pastor*, Eugene Peterson recounts his realization that his ministry was infected with 'the messianic virus'. He had become host to the diseased idea that he was to be the Saviour of his people by attending to every single one of their needs, rather than helping them to be attentive to what God was doing in their lives. *That* was his unique calling as a pastor.[4] Messianic ministry will always be hurried and hassled; legacy-leaving ministry will always be seeking and straining for the next big thing. The people we don't have yet will be loved more than the people we do. Ministry life tomorrow will be better than ministry life today. But that is ministry for me, not others.

I tend to wish my life away at the moment because we have small children at home. I love them very much, of course, but

I do also sometimes think, 'Surely it'll be easier when they're bigger and there are no more tantrums, no more nappies, and rational conversations are the order of the day.' Not long ago I was walking with two of my children, and it was clear to anyone who saw us that things weren't going very well and that Dad was living right on the edge. A neighbour observed us and said to me as we passed, 'These are the best days of your life!' I can assure you it was not what I wanted to hear at the time!

I realized later that my neighbour's proverbial wisdom is exactly the point our Teacher might have made had he accompanied us on our disastrous outing. Stop chasing the wind! Stop thinking the future will be better and easier. Stop thinking that if only things were different you would be a better person and that one day you will be a better father. You do not know the future or what lies around the corner, whether good or ill. Perhaps these are indeed the very best days of my life. Maybe I'll be dead tomorrow.

Live the life you have now instead of longing for the life you think you will have, but which you actually cannot control at all.

When we realize there is a middle way between being lazy in the here and now, and busting a gut for the future, we find tranquillity. We realize that rest and peace are more important than wealth and success. We look down and find that only one hand is full, but we know that it is more than enough. The Puritan preacher Jeremiah Burroughs suggested that we learn to find contentment by way of subtraction rather than addition. People normally think that to achieve contentment you have to attain whatever it is you desire. Our possessions need to be raised up to the level of our desires: 'But the Christian has another way to contentment. He can bring his desires down to his possessions.'[5] G. K. Chesterton is reported to have said exactly the same thing: 'There are two ways to get enough. One is to accumulate more and more. The other is to desire less.'

2 Loving my neighbour, loving myself

Living for we, not me, means a happier, healthier me. The Teacher continues to press this point home in 4:7–8 with another graphic illustration of what life lived for me looks like.

He introduces us to the company chief executive. He's made it all the way to the top of the tree, but he lives there alone. Utterly alone. He has no children, no family, no friends, and his only companions are his work and his wealth. But it's not as if that is enough. His hours are as long now as they've ever been. He obsesses over his emails and meetings and reports. When one bonus arrives, he is thinking of the next one. He can't afford to have a wife and a family, because they would get in the way. A social life would curb his output, and the only input he needs comes from a screen and some figures. 'He could buy dinner for everyone in the restaurant, but no one wants to sit with him. That's all right, because he doesn't want to sit with them either.'[6] So there he is: wealthy but not healthy, alone and lonely, possessing everything except enjoyment. Nothing tastes good any more. As Samuel Johnson said, 'To be unhappy at home is the ultimate result of all ambition.'

It's easy to make a target out of the rich. But the Bible is not against wealth. It is not money that is a root of all kinds of evil, but the love of it (1 Timothy 6:10). Ecclesiastes says exactly the same thing in picture form: it is the two-handed toiling for wealth as an end in itself which is a root of evil. It grows like a strangling vine around the heart, and the harm spreads its tentacles in several different directions at once.

Let me paraphrase an illustration which the American pastor Matt Chandler gives in his sermons on Ecclesiastes. Chandler relates how he has never had a girl come into his office in tears and tell him that she hates her dad because he used to drop her off at school in a beat-up old Ford and it was so embarrassing she has never been able to forgive him. He's never had a girl tell him she hates her dad because he didn't buy her a pony, or send her on the school skiing trip. But he has met plenty of young women whose dad had a $60,000 car, and who could have paid for the whole school to go on the skiing trip, and yet these women have not known the love of their father and so have been given a thoroughly warped perception of their own value.[7]

It is possible to know the price of everything but the value of nothing. If the love of money is a root of evil, then Ecclesiastes – and indeed the whole Bible – has a beautifully simple solution. Here is how to sever the root, stop the rot and kill the evil: spend your money on others. Give it away. Do it regularly, gladly, generously – and you will be happy. Where wealthy people love their neighbour by working for them as much as themselves, and love them with their own hard-earned money, then the beautiful by-product is that they end up loving themselves. They actually provide the best kind of care for themselves because they are no longer alone.

For the Teacher, the value of life is not what you earn, but whom you relate to. It's not what you buy, but what you give. It's there in black and white in 4:9–12. We are given a simple presentation of why two are better than one, and why three are even better than two. If you want to make money, do it with someone else and you might make even more. But at least there's someone to share it with. This is proverbial wisdom in poetic form, a general principle that life lived in community and mutual interdependence is better all round for everyone. Perhaps four are better than three, and so on. We, not me, is always going to be better for me than only me. This is how God designed us to flourish.

So how are you doing with asking *how are we doing*? As you think about where you are going with your life, Ecclesiastes gives you a middle road to walk. Don't hate your neighbour – be neither too lazy to help them nor too powerful to avoid oppressing them; don't be so caught up in your own today that you cannot see their tomorrow. Don't hate yourself – laziness, frenzy, envy and love of money will each in their own way corrode you from the inside out. Take the middle path of loving your neighbour and so properly loving yourself. Don't drop out like the fool; don't be sucked in like the frantic.

Which side of the road are you currently on?

To expose laziness, ask yourself whom you are feeding off, and who is doing the work so that you don't have to. What about giving back to them? If you are an introvert who happily luxuriates in your own company, give one of your afternoons or Saturdays to someone who hates being on their own. Give several of them.

To expose restless striving, ask yourself who it's all really for. It's not that being busy is wrong – far from it – and many of us are busily engaged in doing things for others. But the Teacher simply wants to ask if we are living for ourselves in the midst of all we do. What tasks and jobs might be able to fall by the wayside so that relationships can flourish? I wonder what the impact would be on our families if it were the husbands and dads who every now and then asked the 'how are we doing' question. Have you ever asked it in the church family as you look around on a Sunday morning?

The quest for personal advancement in our fallen world can very quickly inoculate a person against ever looking at the world in this way. It's a picture of the life less upwardly mobile being lived on the middle road. And it is the path to happiness. You do not have as much as you might like, but you know that you have more than you deserve.

As one hand holds, your other one gives.

Questions for discussion or personal reflection

1. Do you think it's true that we spend most of our time thinking about ourselves?
2. How does Ecclesiastes help us to guard against being 'trite and simplistic' as we try to help those immersed in a world of pain (see p. 58)?
3. What are the things which, in your worst moments, you envy in others?
4. Work out how much time you spent working last week, and how much time you spent relaxing with others. Could you spend more/less time on each of those?
5. Who are the 'we's' whom you could start to think about more? Take time to list the practical differences this might make to those relationships.
6. What practical steps can you take to help prevent laziness or being overly busy? What might it look like for you to take the middle road?

5
Looking up, listening in

> *'Better to remain silent and be thought a fool,*
> *than to open your mouth and remove all doubt.'*
> Lisa, *The Simpsons*

Guard your steps when you go to the house of God. Go near to listen rather than to offer the sacrifice of fools, who do not know that they do wrong.

> Do not be quick with your mouth,
>   do not be hasty in your heart
>   to utter anything before God.
> God is in heaven
>   and you are on earth,
>   so let your words be few.
> A dream comes when there are many cares,
>   and many words mark the speech of a fool.

When you make a vow to God, do not delay to fulfil it. He has no pleasure in fools; fulfil your vow. It is better not to make a vow than to make one and not fulfil it. Do not let your mouth lead you into sin. And do not protest to the temple messenger, 'My vow was a mistake.' Why should God be angry at what you

say and destroy the work of your hands? Much dreaming and many words are meaningless. Therefore fear God.
(Ecclesiastes 5:1–7)

'Undivided God seeks undivided worshipper'

The Bible says this is what God is looking for in his world. When the people of Israel were camped on the edge of the Promised Land, Moses preached a sermon to them. His words were to be their travelling instructions, God's requirements for how they should live in the land they were to receive.

> Hear, O Israel: The LORD our God, the LORD is one. Love the LORD your God with all your heart and with all your soul and with all your strength. These commandments that I give you today are to be upon your hearts. Impress them on your children. Talk about them when you sit at home and when you walk along the road, when you lie down and when you get up. Tie them as symbols on your hands and bind them on your foreheads. Write them on the door-frames of your houses and on your gates.
> (Deuteronomy 6:4–9)

There is one, undivided God – 'the LORD our God is one' – and because God is like that, then he must be approached and worshipped by one undivided person: all your heart, all your soul, all your strength. In other words, all of you. Every single bit. God is not pulled in different directions. So neither should we be in our worship of him. Real faith and trust in God are not compartmentalized. He is not looking for people who can give him their strength – mending the church roof or serving in short-term missions – while their greatest loves and deepest desires are directed elsewhere.

If we're honest, we all know what it's like to experience the kind of fragmentation that Moses is warning against. Sometimes everything looks grand on the outside. We're always where we're meant to be, on time and ready to go, always on the rotas and playing our part. But at the core of our beings we know that love for God with heart and soul is absent. We feel dry, he appears distant and a real relationship with him seems out of reach.

So what can we do? In chapter 5 of Ecclesiastes we are given a profound and wise piece of advice: *listen*. In this, the Teacher joins Moses in Deuteronomy and the Lord Jesus himself in the New Testament in saying that the orientation to perfect wholeness as an undivided worshipper starts here. The first word in Deuteronomy 6:4 is 'Hear'. Listen up, Israel! Tune in to what I'm about to tell you. That is why we have graphic images in verses 8 and 9 of tying God's words on hands and foreheads, writing them on door frames of houses. Do that in order to achieve verse 6: God's words upon our hearts. Do whatever you can to help you *listen*, Moses is saying, so that you get what God says in through your ears and lodged in your mental processes and immovably part of who you are as a person. Let his commandments seep into the way you look at the world.

The ear is the Christian's primary sense organ. Listening to what God has said is our main spiritual discipline. We need someone to tell us to listen because we want to look and speak more than we want to listen. When it comes to relating to God, we are out of order as far as using our sense organs goes. The things we see and the things we can touch dominate the way we perceive reality. We are fundamentally active creatures. We are what we do. But Ecclesiastes says that we become more human when we are what we receive. Life is a gift, and God's Word is the most precious of gifts, to be honoured and loved and treasured above all others. Ecclesiastes is one long meditation on the need to use our ears for God's Word alongside our eyes in God's world.

If you simply look at the world of human activity, what do you see? Remember Ecclesiastes 4. you see oppression and toil, and the tears of the crushed with no one to comfort them. As you look at the world of human wisdom and learning, what do you see? Lecture series after lecture series, seminar after seminar, everyone sitting round in little cliques spouting about this and that, and most of it driven by envy of neighbour, a desire to show you're as bright as the next person and have read a book they haven't. Most of it is simply waffling in the wind. The world eludes our control and it eludes the explanation of our best minds. No one can really explain exactly how the brain works, or why we humans sometimes behave in the most unpredictable of ways. No one will finally come up with a solution to world poverty or to all forms of injustice. The Teacher is saying that looking at the world, and speaking about the world, will only get you so far – so are we all doomed? Should we shut up shop and go home?

No, he says to us in Ecclesiastes 5, all is not lost. If you're despairing about life, the universe and everything, then use your ears. The Teacher is re-preaching what Moses preached in Deuteronomy: 'Hear, O Israel.' He is giving us a sermon about how human beings may not be able to read the book of creation (the world), but we can read the book of the Law (the Bible). It is a fallen world, and interpreting it to our complete satisfaction cannot be done. You cannot always read it. But you can read the Bible. And as you read, God is speaking. So listen.

Ecclesiastes is always constructing the same world-view for us. A consistent picture is being painted, and this time the brush strokes sketch the importance of God's speech more fully than we have seen so far.

1 Listening to God (verses 1–3)

'Guard your steps when you go to the house of God. Go near to listen rather than to offer the sacrifice of fools, who do not know that they do wrong' (5:1). If Ecclesiastes is like a photo album, with snapshots of activity and hustle and bustle in the world, images of grief and pain and wealth and success, here in chapter 5 the camera lens turns on the religious worshipper. There is just as much to see here, and, if you're into this sort of thing, the images are really spectacular.

Worship services can be so impressive. Think of the ones you see on *Songs of Praise*. Picture in your mind a church packed with worshippers in full flow and good voice. The camera catches all the right angles in the magnificent cathedral: the stunning architecture, the candles, the stained-glass windows, the beautiful artefacts. *Songs of Praise* always comes with a gentle host, who introduces it all while smiling nicely and speaking lovely words about the church and the people and the wonderful setting. 'Ah,' they say, as the hymn ends and we cut back to them standing outside or sitting in their comfortable armchair, 'what truly moving words they are, what an exquisite rendition that was.'

But the Teacher in Ecclesiastes is a very different kind of host. He too is introducing us to remarkable worship services, but he is not gentle and he is not about to use lovely words. He is a host who leads us into the church, shows us the service in all its pomp and glory, and then as the camera switches back to him, he looks us right in the eye and says, 'If that is all there is, then what a load of claptrap! What a waste of time! These folks might as well be at home tidying the garden shed for all God cares!'

The Bible deals with hypocrisy in different ways. The prophets hurl invective, crying, 'How dare you behave like this!' Ecclesiastes takes a surgeon's scalpel and quietly turns it on the well-meaning person who likes a good sing and who turns up cheerfully enough to worship, but who listens only with ears half-open. They listen like this because they think they know it all, and what they think and what they have to say is more interesting and important than what God says. This kind of worship is mere verbal doodling. Any television camera looking at it would leave you thinking how lovely it is. But God looks at it and calls the people doing it fools. He sees through the charade.

When verse 1 says that such fools 'do not know that they do wrong', it's referring to the kind of person who has become so used to playing games with God that they no longer expect religion to be anything else. The sham is normal. It's just the way it is, and there's been no lightning bolt from heaven, so it must be fine to keep trundling along like this.

In the Old Testament everything about the temple was designed to help the worshipper realize that this wouldn't work. It was a majestic building to teach God's people that they had a majestic God. It dwarfed you in size in order to teach you that God was bigger than you, so much more than you could take in or comprehend. It was meant to make you look up and see how small you were. But if you forget to look up and just start looking around, then you simply get into the habit of bringing your sacrifice and forgetting about your heart. You soon forget that God sees everything.

The teacher's knife cuts very deeply here. Just pause to ask: why is this material in chapter 5 placed straight after chapter 4? Why are we now being told to listen after everything we looked at in the previous chapter? We are meant to see that we haven't changed topics at all because both chapters are about worship. Chapter 4 was all about the worship of wealth and self-advancement and the problems that causes for me and my neighbour when I pursue those goals. Chapter 5 simply sets true worship, the kind of worship that reveals authenticity, against false worship. Jesus said, 'No one can serve two masters. Either you will hate the one and love the other, or you will be devoted to the one and despise the other. You cannot serve both God and Money' (Matthew 6:24).

One God – the real God, the living God – commands love of him and love of my neighbour. The other gods – wealth, success, achievement, advancement – command trampling on my neighbour to get what I want. And in the Bible, from start to end, from the prophets to the apostle Paul, there is a constant critique of those who oppress their neighbour and serve only themselves, and yet turn up at the prayer meeting saying everything's fine. The Teacher looks us in the eye: watch out! Be careful! You need to know that approaching God can be dangerous if you're approaching him thinking he couldn't care less what is really happening in your heart, and about how you're treating your spouse or your colleagues or your family member.

Don't be too quick just to tell God what you think he wants to hear. That's what verse 2 means. Someone has said that when we pray we tend to think it's like talking into a spiritual microphone with God listening on the other end through a set of heavenly earphones. But, in fact, when we pray, God is listening to us with a spiritual stethoscope. Just like the doctor who says, 'Let me hear you breathe', and he listens in to what we cannot see and so learns the truth about us. God is in heaven. Can't you see, as you look around, how small you are and how big God is? So don't you think his stethoscope is always working? Don't shoot off your mouth or speak before you think. Ecclesiastes is teaching us that we need God's Word, we need his revelation about who he is and what he's like, in order to reverence him properly.

So are you listening? Are you listening more than you're speaking? In the context of this passage, the fool is the religious person who thinks they have all the answers. They're the kind of person who comes alongside a struggling friend and confidently tells them what to do. Their wounded friend is wondering why God has allowed a terrible thing to happen, or why God seems so distant in this time of anguish. The fool comes alongside and claims to have all the answers, and behaving as if they can unlock all the riddles of the world.

We are often slow – I know I am – to direct our own hearts, or folks we speak with, to what God has said. That kind of approach with a struggling friend starts with humble awareness of the profound fact that God is in heaven and I am on earth, and I'm unlikely to understand this mess any more than you do. But in our confusion we have words to read which tell us who God is and what he has done and what he will one day do. There are always words from him to listen to, whatever circumstances we may find ourselves in.

Fools gush out their own words instead of listening for God's words. Verse 3 uses an illustration to press the point:

> A dream comes when there are many cares,
>   and many words mark the speech of a fool.

It's a clever picture because it ties in so well with the argument of the whole book so far. By saying that dreams come from overwork, the Teacher is making the point that 'it is as natural for the fool to be verbose as it is for dreams to come to those who toil pointlessly for gain'. Iain Provan captures this perfectly: 'Overproduction is the root problem in both cases. A heart attentive to God multiplies neither toil nor words.'[1]

2 Speaking to God (verses 4–7)

If the way of wisdom is listening to God more, and pontificating to him or to others about him less, how then should we speak to him?

In verse 4 the teacher now comes to focus in on *our* speech to God, and at first glance it seems a little remote from us. Making vows probably isn't something that we do often, but there's a very simple principle here which is part of living wisely in God's world. When you tell God you'll do something, do it. He takes no pleasure in foolish chatter. Vow it, and then do it. Far better not to promise in the first place than to vow and not pay up. Don't let your mouth make a sinner out of you (verse 6).

Now what is the Teacher saying? In this part of the photo album, as we look at the religious worshipper, Ecclesiastes is showing us the kind of person who looks at the world and realizes that it is beyond her control, beyond her complete comprehension – and because of that, decides it doesn't really matter what she does, says, thinks, or feels in her heart. She can say whatever she wants and waffle away as much as she likes about God. She can even say whatever she wants to God, because if she can't always see the meaning of the world, then her own words have no meaning.

Consider the person who says, 'Lord, I'm in a really tight corner here, but if you get me out of it, I promise I'll serve you with my whole life!' And then the crisis passes, and of course they never give God a second thought. Why? Because, well, God's probably not really there; the person was just stuck and needed something to say. It's just words.

But here in Ecclesiastes, for the believer, this kind of attitude is extremely serious. God is in heaven. God will bring to judgment both the righteous and the wicked. God sees and hears and knows everything. And the Teacher says to us: the one, undivided God wants an undivided worshipper. A worshipper who is not saying 'yes, yes' over here and 'no, no' over there. Someone who says what they mean and means what they say.

Vows like this in verses 4–6 were never commanded in Old Testament law, but they were permitted, and they always came with the proviso that you would do what you said. When we see what Jesus said about vows in the New Testament, we realize that although vows were not commanded, they were permitted, and yet they should not be necessary:

> But I tell you, do not swear an oath at all: either by heaven, for it is God's throne; or by the earth, for it is his footstool; or by Jerusalem, for it is the city of the Great King. And do not swear by your head, for you cannot make even one hair white or black. All you need to say is simply 'Yes,' or 'No'; anything beyond this comes from the evil one.
> (Matthew 5:34–37)

Vows, oaths and swearing all exist because we're untruthful. We naturally shave the edges off what really happened, and shade the details as we fill someone in. Because we all know that, we tend to prefix certain things we say with vows:

'Honestly, I'm telling you the truth. Here's what she said . . .'

'No word of a lie, this is what happened . . .'

If you just tell a lie, plain and simple, that's bad. But if you actually preface your lie by saying, 'I swear to tell the truth, the whole truth and nothing but the truth', then that's even worse. For you have wrapped your untruthfulness inside a pledge of your truthfulness.

When we stop to think about it and realize that God is in heaven and sees into our hearts, what do you think we look like to God with all our speech, all our words, if our speech bears little connection to reality? That's what the Teacher is saying to us. If you think it's bad not to do something, then how much worse is it not to do it after you've promised God you'll do it?

So the principle here is very helpful: when you speak to God, or when you speak to others, simplicity safeguards your sincerity. Believers who are simply honest do not need to resort to vows, or oaths of any kind. An unadorned 'yes' or 'no' protects the sincerity of your speaking. We become people without flowery pretence, without angles and edges that need to be negotiated by others. What you see is what you get. We become people like this when we decide that because God sees, I am not going to live off the fact that the person I am speaking to does not see.

So we can see that the issue of making vows is not irrelevant to us. It is simply an application of the reality of God to everyday life. You may not know whether I'm telling the truth – but God does. When I live with the reality of God, the God in heaven who has my heart open before him like an open book, I stand in awe of him (verse 7), and this takes concrete form in the kind of words which do and do not leave my mouth.

Thinking it through

We each have different ways of not listening to God. Some of us are confident types, and we've either got plenty to say to explain theology or plenty to say to question things. Well, asks the Teacher, is there more coming in than going out? Who appointed you as a leading authority under the sun on such and such a topic? Last time I looked, says the Teacher, God knew more about it than both of us.

Others of us are of a different type. Rather than having too many words to say to God, we sometimes feel like we don't have any words, never mind too many. Maybe it's because we don't know what to say to God. Maybe we want to say to the Teacher in Ecclesiastes, 'You don't understand *my* problem. I'm desperate to hear, to listen, but God just doesn't seem to be saying anything.' That can be such a struggle. It's all very well me being silent – but what about when God seems silent?

Anyone who has walked the path of faith will tell you that life under the sun can often be like this, and there are rarely any easy answers. But the Teacher does say this to us: the reality of God is measured by the truthfulness of his speech, not by my grasp of his presence. Under the sun sometimes everything is so mixed up and back to front that actually we are meant to learn that God intends for us to be suspicious of ourselves – suspicious of why we doubt him and why we cannot find him, suspicious of the deceptions of our own hearts – but nevertheless trusting the truth of his Word with every fibre of our being, even when we cannot see him.

It has always been so for God's people. It's interesting that in Deuteronomy 5 the people say to Moses, 'Go near and listen to all that the LORD our God says. Then tell us whatever the LORD our God tells you. We will listen and obey' (verse 27). They have no sight of God, and receive no personal encounter with him face to face (they know that to do this would mean their destruction). But instead of sight, there is sound. God speaks, and the only correct response is to say, 'We will listen and obey.'

You and I take our place under the sun in exactly the same way. God has spoken. And we can choose how to respond.

Questions for discussion or personal reflection

1. Do you listen well? Does speech come easily?
2. In what contexts might we be at risk of being 'quick with our mouths' and 'hasty in heart' before God?
3. When did you last break a promise to someone else? According to Ecclesiastes, what would the impact have been of fulfilling that promise?
4. 'God is in heaven'; 'Fear God.' Why is it so easy to lose this perspective and this attitude?
5. 'Simplicity safeguards sincerity' (see p. 78). Can you think of any changes you could make to your speech that could put this principle into action in your life?

6

Learning to love the limitations of life

*'We need to be alienated from what we think we know
in order to genuinely grow.'*
Brian Brock, *Captive to Christ, Open to the World*

A good name is better than fine perfume,
    and the day of death better than the day of birth.
It is better to go to a house of mourning
    than to go to a house of feasting,
for death is the destiny of everyone;
    the living should take this to heart.
Frustration is better than laughter,
    because a sad face is good for the heart.
The heart of the wise is in the house of mourning,
    but the heart of fools is in the house of pleasure.
It is better to heed the rebuke of a wise person
    than to listen to the song of fools.
Like the crackling of thorns under the pot,
    so is the laughter of fools.
    This too is meaningless.

Extortion turns a wise man into a fool,
> and a bribe corrupts the heart.

The end of a matter is better than its beginning,
> and patience is better than pride.

Do not be quickly provoked in your spirit,
> for anger resides in the lap of fools.

Do not say, 'Why were the old days better than these?'
> For it is not wise to ask such questions.

Wisdom, like an inheritance, is a good thing
> and benefits those who see the sun.

Wisdom is a shelter
> as money is a shelter,

but the advantage of knowledge is this:
> wisdom preserves those who have it.

Consider what God has done:

Who can straighten
> what he has made crooked?

When times are good, be happy;
> but when times are bad, consider this:

God has made the one
> as well as the other.

Therefore, no one can discover
> anything about their future.

In this meaningless life of mine I have seen both of these:

the righteous perishing in their righteousness,
> and the wicked living long in their wickedness.

Do not be over-righteous,
>   neither be overwise –
>   why destroy yourself?
Do not be overwicked,
>   and do not be a fool –
>   why die before your time?
It is good to grasp the one
>   and not let go of the other.
>   Whoever fears God will avoid all extremes.

Wisdom makes one wise person more powerful
>   than ten rulers in a city.

Indeed, there is no one on earth who is righteous,
>   no one who does what is right and never sins.

Do not pay attention to every word people say,
>   or you may hear your servant cursing you –
for you know in your heart
>   that many times you yourself have cursed others.

All this I tested by wisdom and I said,

'I am determined to be wise' –
>   but this was beyond me.
Whatever exists is far off and most profound –
>   who can discover it?
So I turned my mind to understand,
>   to investigate and to search out wisdom and the scheme
>   of things
and to understand the stupidity of wickedness
>   and the madness of folly.

(Ecclesiastes 7:1–25)

Wisdom vs escapism

Once we grasp the big message of Ecclesiastes – that life in this world eludes our control – how then should we live?

There are two options. When we realize that we cannot explain everything, that the people we love will become ill and die, and we don't know why God could allow this to happen, once we accept there is injustice and oppression, or we have to face the fact that there is a throbbing hurt at the core of our soul that won't go away, one option is to try to flee reality and numb the pain to avoid the problems. Party as hard as we can, laugh as loud and as often as possible, drink ourselves into oblivion, live in the past or a land of make-believe instead of the present. That's the route of escapism.

The other option, the one on offer here in Ecclesiastes 7, is wisdom. Learn to live wisely in God's world in the midst of all the brokenness. But there's a big surprise with this alternative. The wisest thing you can do is to realize that not even being wise will tell you everything you want to know.

The message of the chapter is this: be neither an escapist, nor a theological snob. For part of living wisely is learning to live with the limitations of wisdom itself. This is a consistent theme in the Bible's wisdom literature. It is what Job understood:

> Where then does wisdom come from?
>   Where does understanding dwell?
> It is hidden from the eyes of every living thing,
>   concealed even from the birds in the sky.
> Destruction and Death say,
>   'Only a rumour of it has reached our ears.'
> God understands the way to it
>   and he alone knows where it dwells.
> (Job 28:20–23)

So you think you've got wisdom? You think you've got your life in order, got it nailed down, you think you understand how the world works? If death and destruction come knocking on your door on a Tuesday morning completely out of the blue, if the doctor tells you that your own end is near or the phone rings with heart-breaking news, then at that moment you will realize the control you thought you had over life was just self-deception. Thinking you know enough to have control of your own life is just an illusion, but the tears on your pillow at night are real. When we try to get a fully satisfying handle on how things work, we discover that wisdom seems to live on the other side of the world. We chase it, but we just can't get the full measure of it.

So look, the Teacher says to us in this chapter, you can learn to love the fact that life is limited in this way. All the pithy sayings of Ecclesiastes 7 are like little gems, each powerful in their own way, but they aren't randomly arranged or completely disconnected from one another. They are each here to set out an alternative way of living under the sun once we see that controlling every part of our lives is impossible.

There are two parts to the chapter. First, we need to realize that as we go through life, death is holding out an invitation to us. Second, as we go through life we need to realize that wisdom is good: it's sensible, it's upright, it's often beautiful – but God has limited our grasp of it.

1 *The invitation of death (verses 1–6)*
These verses tell us that life is limited by death. Your life won't go on for ever. But death is not just a line you cross when your time is up. Death is an evangelist. He looks us in the eye and asks us to look him right back with a steady gaze and allow him to do his work in us. Death is a preacher with a very simple message. Death has an invitation for us. He wants to

teach us that the day of our coming death can be a friend to us in advance. The very limitation which death introduces into our life can instruct us about life. Think of it as death's helping hand.

Look how the Teacher makes this point: 'A good name is better than fine perfume' (verse 1). We understand this and we think it's a lovely proverb. There's no point smelling like a bed of roses if every time your name is mentioned at the dinner party people feel the emotional equivalent of nails screeching down a blackboard. Don't be the kind of person who makes others wince, even though outwardly you look great. No – your reputation, your character, the things you are known for – these things are so much more important than mere superficial trivia. So far so good.

But look at the second half of the verse. In just the same way, 'the day of death [is] better than the day of birth' (verse 1). Maternity wards can be some of the happiest places on earth. Even if we haven't experienced it for ourselves, we can imagine the joy a baby brings. All that life, all that hope, all that potential stretching ahead: so how can the day of death ever be better than the day of birth?

We might think the clue is in that word 'potential'. Birth is all about potential, but death, for the believer, is all about fulfilment. A Christian parent might have hopes and dreams and prayers for their children, but at the moment of death, and only at that moment, does anyone perfectly receive all that Christ has won for them. Death is the fulfilment of life, and fulfilment is better than potential. That is a rich reading of this verse, and it's certainly in line with the rest of the Bible. But I think our writer means something different.

In my opinion, the Teacher is saying that the day of your death is a better teacher than the day of your birth. When a new baby is born, there is virtually nothing we can say about her, beyond vague impressions of physical resemblance to one of the parents or grandparents. 'Oh,' we say, 'she's so like her mum.' Possibly. But that's about it.

Now fast forward to the day of that baby's death. Aged eighty-six. What can we say about her then?

'She was so like Jesus.'

'She was so kind, so generous. What depth there was to her as a person.'

Or:

'She loved her garden.'

'She loved her knitting.'

'She loved her bingo.'

'She loved . . .'

You choose something to fill in the blank that really isn't very much at all.

'She didn't really love anything or anyone very much apart from herself.'

'She lived for herself alone.'

The day of death is better than the day of birth – not because death is better than life; it's not – but because a coffin is a better preacher than a cot. When life ends, or is about to end, absolutely everything else comes into focus. The things that don't really matter, but which we gave so much time to, now seem so empty and pointless. The lives we touched and the generosity we showed and the love we gave or received now mean so much more. That's what the Teacher is saying: a coffin preaches better sermons than a cot. 'Look forward,' he says as he grabs us by the shoulders. 'Don't be a fool! Stop trying to escape life's agonies by drowning them away, by laughing them off and pretending they don't exist. Look forward to the day of your death and ask yourself, what kind of person should I be? For one day I will be dead.'

It is better to go to a house of mourning
  than to go to a house of feasting,
for death is the destiny of everyone;
  the living should take this to heart.
(verse 2)

The heart of the wise is in the house of mourning,
  but the heart of fools is in the house of pleasure.
(verse 4)

The Teacher has learnt that there are two types of people at the funeral in the crematorium. The fool sits there thinking how unbearably grim this is, and can't wait to be outside in the sunshine and back to what he was doing, and to get out to the pub in the evening. But the wise person sits in the crematorium and stares at the coffin, and realizes that one day it will be his turn. The wise person asks himself, 'When it is my turn, what will my life have been worth? What will they be saying about me?' He loved his bowling and his partying and his holidays. Is that it?

I've been to some parties, says the Teacher, and you wouldn't believe the half of it if I told you about them, but I tell you this: I never met anyone drinking themselves under the table who was dealing with life's big issues. Listen, he says, better to have a friend sit and list out all your faults in front of you than to spend your life trying to be on *The X Factor* (verse 5). The Teacher says he's never met a wise pop star, but he has seen many others discover wisdom at their funerals. Laughter, pleasure – well, nothing wrong with them in themselves, of course – but amusement like that disappears as quickly as kindling sticks when you start a fire (verse 6). But, says the Teacher, let me tell you this: I put my life in order when I went to the crematorium. When I went, death said to me, 'Come in and stay a while. Have a seat and stop and think.' And I listened to what death said to me.

It's very important to be clear: the person who lives like this is not morbid. On the contrary, what characterizes a person who lives like this is depth: they have depth of soul, depth of character. But superficiality is the mark of the escapist who is living in denial. The tag line to the film *Fame* is 'I'm gonna live forever'. But it was the tag line to the original film many years ago, only this time with different actors – because they don't live for ever. They've now got cellulite and their legs don't do what they used to do, so we need new younger, prettier dancers who are going to live for ever. And so it goes on.

If you live in denial of death, what is there to do but eat and laugh and drink and party? Instead of being superficial, death invites you to be a person of depth. Only someone who knows how to weep will really know what it means to laugh. That's the message of Ecclesiastes. It's an invitation to be a person who realizes that living a good life means preparing to die a good death.

Have you ever met someone like this? They're the kind of person who is actually fully alive, engaged with the world and their family and the goodness of creation because they know that they have it all on loan – it's a gift – and that one day God will simply call time, but when he does, they're ready to go. Will you let death teach you the limitations of your life? Will you let it reshape your goals, your attitudes, the things you long for and work for and pray for and hope for the most? For if death is not your lord and does not own you – it never, ever can be if you are in Christ – then it can teach you.

And it is not only our own future death which can teach us. We can learn from death through the ways others have already been deeply shaped by it. No one who tastes death up close and personal is ever the same again.

One night in the autumn of 1991, in rural Idaho, Gerald Sittser was driving with his wife, his four children and his mother, when their car was struck by a drunk driver and, in a moment, he lost his wife, mother and four-year-old daughter. In the aftermath, Sittser wrote a beautiful and profoundly moving book on loss and sorrow called *A Grace Disguised*.[1] His reflections portray an unspeakable agony from the inside, while powerfully describing how he and his surviving children slowly began to piece their lives back together again.

Eight years after *A Grace Disguised* was first published, Sittser had the opportunity to comment on how far he and his children had come in the time since the accident. In the Preface to the second edition of his book, he reveals that his 'rawness and utter bewilderment . . . have given way to contentment and deep gratitude'. His story has turned out to be 'redemptive, not only for me and my children, but for many other people as well'. And then he says, 'As strange as it might sound, I wish that every man could experience what I have, though without the acute suffering.'[2] That Sittser was ever able to describe his trauma as a grace disguised is remarkable; but that he is now standing in a place where he has received the kind of gifts from it which he wishes others could share is surely a profound surprise. You will need to read his book to see what these gifts are.

People who survive catastrophic loss often say that they survived by coming to see, in time, that they somehow had to take the loss into themselves and allow it to enlarge their heart so that their capacity to live well and to enjoy simple things and to know God intimately increased in a way they never thought possible. It is as if God somehow stretches a person to breaking point, and then they discover that because they have been stretched, there is now room in their heart and mind for God and for life and for others, which was not there before. Gerald Sittser even writes of the sickness of the soul which can 'only be healed through suffering'.[3]

Death has the capacity to teach us things about love and joy that we could only learn because of death, but it does not mean that the experience of learning them is lovely or joyful. Nicholas Wolterstorff's meditations in *Lament for a Son* on the death of his twenty-five-year-old son in a climbing accident are the most moving evocations of grief I have read.[4] I wept when I read them for the first time, and then guiltily felt somehow voyeuristic for entering the emotions of shattering loss without experiencing the loss itself. Recently, however, I noticed at the start of his book that Wolterstorff comments on another father's strange habit of giving this book to each of his children. He does so because it is a love letter. That is precisely why it is so powerful and so painful: lament expresses love. Someone else's lament can give voice not just to your own grief, but also to your love. It can teach you the language of your heart, which you did not know you knew.

Death dons a preacher's robe to teach us that life is finite and we must use it well. It leans down from a pulpit to impress on us that those whom we love are finite, that we love them more deeply than we realize, and that we must love them well. The sermons death preaches – if we choose our sermons wisely – can tell us more about the way we love and the way we live than we ever realize is actually going on while we love and live.

2 The limitation of wisdom (verses 7–25)
It's important to grasp the balanced view the Teacher is giving us. He tried to use wisdom to test everything he saw in the

world, and it just left him bewildered when he couldn't tie up all the loose ends (verse 23). But that doesn't mean that wisdom is useless. Certain courses of action are better than others. He gives us four examples: extortion, impatience, anger and nostalgia. We'll look at the first three briefly and linger more over the fourth.

Money
Be alert to the danger of extortion (verse 7). Wisdom does not come in stainless steel – it can rust, it can go bad, it can go off. In other words, even a wise person can be reduced to being a fool when the pound signs flash. Everyone has their price, so the saying goes. But the Teacher says to us: you must prove the saying wrong. Do not be the kind of person who can be bought.

You can stop your heart being corrupted by going to the crematorium and listening to death's sermon about money. Extra cash? What are you going to do with it? You could always use it to line the walls of your coffin.

Let your coming death protect your heart.

Patience
To see a project through to its end is better than to be the kind of person who starts and never finishes (verse 8). Patience is a virtue. Anything worthwhile takes time to develop and grow. So give it the time it needs.

Anger
If you adopt the long-term view, you're going to come up against serious frustrations, so do some exercises to lengthen your fuse. Attend a funeral and realize that one day you'll be dead too. Is it really worth being the kind of person who loses their rag? If you do, you are a fool (verse 9).

Nostalgia

> Do not say, 'Why were the old days better than these?'
> For it is not wise to ask such questions.
>
> (verse 10)

It's very common to hear this sentiment today, almost word for word:

'Things aren't like they used to be.'

'Why is the world getting so bad? Violent crime is on the rise.'

'I'm glad I didn't have to bring up my children in these days.'

But here's how I think the Teacher in Ecclesiastes would respond to people who say things like this: if you think you're living in a world where things are getting worse all the time, then cheer up: at least you'll be dead before things get *really* bad.

Maybe the past was better than the present. But when you start asking, '*Why* was it better?', what you are doing is denying the reality of God's presence in the present. If you think things are worse, do you think God is no longer in control now? Do you think he hasn't brought you to the point where you are now and that he no longer loves you or has plans or purposes for you? To ask the question in verse 10 is unwise, because it forgets about God. Often when we ask this, it's because we are blind to the good things of the present and ignorant of the evil of the past.

Notice how each of these four things are all variations on escapism. Extortion is a way of escaping your responsibility; impatience is a way of escaping reality and wishing things were different from the way they are; anger is a way of escaping your inability to cope with things not being the way you want them. Nostalgia is a form of escapism by taking a holiday in the past instead of grappling with the present or looking to the future in faith.

But let's pause here to think a little bit more about nostalgia. We will do so with the help of C. S. Lewis. Nostalgia is something that affects all of us, not just older people looking back wistfully at their youth. Perhaps we get nostalgic about buildings or places; most likely, we experience nostalgia for people or an intensity of emotion we felt at a particular time. Have you ever stopped to think about the feeling of nostalgia and what it actually is?

C. S. Lewis said that nostalgia is the special emotion of longing and it is always bittersweet. When we feel nostalgia, we experience a feeling of something lost, and yet at the same time it is a beautiful perception of what has been lost, and so we long for it. Nostalgia is often fleeting, and yet if there is any pain, there is also a kind of satisfying longing as part of it. Now here's what Lewis says: only children or the emotionally immature think that the thing they think they are longing for is actually what they are longing for. The child thinks his memory of that beautiful hillside gives him a lovely feeling so that if he could go back to that hillside he would have the lovely feeling all over again and for as long as he stayed there. No, says Lewis, that is simply unwise. When you mature, you realize that nostalgia plays a kind of trick on you. It intensifies your emotions. When you grow up, you realize that if you could go back to the hillside, it might be nice, it might be lovely, but it would also be ordinary in some ways, and simply going back to it would not generate that intensity of feeling.

> The books or the music in which we thought the beauty was located will betray us if we trust to them; for it was not *in* them, it only came *through* them, and what came through them was

longing. These things – the beauty, the memory of our own past – are good images of what we really desire; but if they are mistaken for the thing itself, they turn into dumb idols, breaking the hearts of their worshippers. For they are not the thing itself; they are only the scent of a flower we have not found, the echo of a tune we have not heard, news from a far country we have not yet visited.[5]

When you experience nostalgia, your heart is longing for a more beautiful person than you have ever met or a more beautiful place than you have ever known. You think you're longing for the past; but the past was never as good as your mind is telling you it was. And, says Lewis, God is giving you in that moment one of the most profound glimpses of the intensity of perfection and beauty that you have actually yet to see. What is in fact pulling on your heartstrings is the future: it's heaven; it's your sense of home and belonging that has just cracked the surface of your life, for just a moment, and then is gone.

This fits beautifully with the message of Ecclesiastes. Remember what we saw in chapter 3. God has placed eternity in our hearts. We're built for home, for a place we cannot see yet, and so when we get that flashing moment of nostalgia, it's like tiny pinpricks of that eternal home breaking through into our present life. The wise person who understands how God has made us to long for him and for heaven doesn't look backwards when they get nostalgic. They allow the feeling to point forwards. They look up to heaven and to home.

So it's clear that wisdom has benefits. But now notice 7:13. Wisdom has definite limits. Wisdom cannot straighten out what God has made crooked, cannot explain why gangsters drive sports cars and good people go hungry and die poor. Why does God allow it? We don't know.

Wisdom can actually be dangerous. A little wisdom can go a long way, or a little wisdom can be enough to hang yourself with if you forget that the world is twisted by sin and every heart is affected, and so we can't fully explain everything. Wisdom can never achieve for human beings the kind of control over your life and destiny that you seek. It can help you with your money, with your impatience, with your anger, with nostalgia. It can help you not to be too upset when you listen at the door and hear something you wished you hadn't (verse 21), because if you're wise, you'll realize that you often say those sorts of things about others. Wisdom can help you like that.

But never forget that it is God who controls the times. It is God who rules the universe. And so although you can live well, and die well, and know some things truly, you cannot know all things completely.

But God does. So trust him – and do not make an idol out of wisdom.

Questions for discussion or personal reflection

1. Why do we find it so difficult to love the fact that life has limitations?
2. When was the last time you went to a funeral? How did you feel? What can you learn from that?
3. This chapter has argued that death is a teacher with an invitation. Explain what that means in your own words.
4. Anger, impatience, greed, nostalgia – what impact should death have on each of these in our lives?
5. Which of these things do you need to ask God to help you deal with more wisely?

7

From death to depth

'What is the meaning of all this gluttony, this waste, this self-indulgence? Where did you get all these things?'
The White Witch, *The Lion, the Witch and the Wardrobe*

So I reflected on all this and concluded that the righteous and the wise and what they do are in God's hands, but no one knows whether love or hate awaits them. All share a common destiny – the righteous and the wicked, the good and the bad, the clean and the unclean, those who offer sacrifices and those who do not.

As it is with the good,
    so with the sinful;
as it is with those who take oaths,
    so with those who are afraid to take them.

This is the evil in everything that happens under the sun:
The same destiny overtakes all. The hearts of people, moreover, are full of evil and there is madness in their hearts while they live, and afterwards they join the dead. Anyone who is among the living has hope – even a live dog is better off than a dead lion!

For the living know that they will die,
    but the dead know nothing;

they can have no further reward,
    and even their name is forgotten.
Their love, their hate
    and their jealousy have long since vanished;
never again will they have a part
    in anything that happens under the sun.

Go, eat your food with gladness, and drink your wine with a joyful heart, for God has already approved what you do. Always be clothed in white, and always anoint your head with oil. Enjoy life with your wife, whom you love, all the days of this meaningless life that God has given you under the sun – all your meaningless days. For this is your lot in life and in your toilsome labour under the sun. Whatever your hand finds to do, do it with all your might, for in the realm of the dead, where you are going, there is neither working nor planning nor knowledge nor wisdom.

    I have seen something else under the sun:

The race is not to the swift
    or the battle to the strong,
nor does food come to the wise
    or wealth to the brilliant
    or favour to the learned;
but time and chance happen to them all.

Moreover, no one knows when their hour will come:

As fish are caught in a cruel net,
    or birds are taken in a snare,
so people are trapped by evil times
    that fall unexpectedly upon them.
(Ecclesiastes 9:1–12)

Killing me not-so-softly

It's clear from verse 1 that we are now reaching the end of Ecclesiastes. It's time for the Teacher to spell out his conclusions and lessons learned. There are actually four more chapters to go in Ecclesiastes, but by taking his time to state his findings, he allows us to catch our breath. Some of what he has been telling us is so unusual, so outside the box from the way we normally think, or even from the way we normally think of the Bible, that it's as if he knows we need time to marinate in it. Often my wife has to tell me four or five times what's going on before I get it into my thick head. We're really no different when the Bible tells us about life as it really is.

In this chapter the Teacher offers another chance to look at his picture of life in God's world. Death, and the inexplicable nature of life – that is, why do the good sometimes die young while the evil live to a ripe old age – and the fact that things seem out of kilter, the joys of food and wine: all these things are on display again for us in this chapter. But so too is a really unusual lens through which the writer views all of them. Here's his lens: 'Go, eat your food with gladness, and drink your wine with a joyful heart, for God has already approved what you do' (verse 7). What are we to make of this?

This verse is actually the book of Ecclesiastes in a nutshell. It reveals the way in which the Teacher looks at the world as we know it, and takes us to the heart of his purpose in writing Ecclesiastes. He wrote his book to smash into tiny pieces our idea that we can be like God. We aspire to have it all, know it all, do it all, achieve it all, be happy for ever, have all the answers, never be left scratching our head, and be remembered by all for all time. That's what we hope for. But what guarantee is there that we won't go under a bus tomorrow?

If you knew that would happen to you tomorrow, how would you live *today* – that is the whole point of Ecclesiastes. The life you have today comes from God's hand as a gift. You have it for a short while, and one day God will call time and take it back. Enjoy life with your wife today because tomorrow she might be gone – or you might be.

In this chapter the Teacher uses three different hammers to shatter our illusions that we can control our own lives, that we can be gods and decide our destinies. To destroy our idolatries he shows us one thing in life which is certain (verses 1–6); he shows us many things in life which are not certain (verses 11–12); and then sandwiched in between them he shows us the simple things in life which are wise (verses 7–10). In what follows, I'm going to take the two bookends first. These are the two big hammer blows that wake us up out of our false notions about the world being neat and tidy and explainable. In the middle, the Teacher presents us with the alternative way to live.

1 The one thing in life which is certain (verses 1–6)

Yet again the Teacher asks us to look long and hard and carefully at the one thing in life which is certain: our death. In a broken and fallen and messed-up world, it's an incredibly stark reality that the only thing we can depend on for sure is that we are closer to the point of our death right now than when we first started to read this book. The Teacher is wrestling with the fact that death comes to us all, no matter who we are or what we've done. No one knows whether love or hate lie ahead, but what we do know is that there is one end for everyone. Righteous and wicked, good people, bad people, the nice and the nasty, believer and unbeliever, the honest truth-teller and the lying deceiver – all go into the ground at the end.

When the Teacher says in verse 3, 'This is the evil in everything that happens under the sun', he's not just saying that death is the evil, although that's true. He's saying that the way death does its work is also evil. It takes the good along with the bad, and where is the justice in that? It makes no sense. For anyone to experience death is an outrage. It is not the way the world was meant to be. Yet how much bigger an outrage it is when you see a young person cut down in their prime. If you expect good people to get a fair deal from the grim reaper, then you have a very bitter pill to swallow. This is not the way the world is at all.

Now notice the writer's perspective: under the sun, this is an evil. Why should the drug dealer and mass murderer receive the same as the upright? Under the sun it does not make sense. Notice the Teacher is not saying that there is no sense at all. He's just saying that *to us* it does not make sense: the righteous and the wise and what they do are in God's hands.

When you put these two things together – God knows the big picture that we do not know, and what we know of our little picture is that death is the certain end for us, whoever we are and whatever we've done – then life is worth living. 'Anyone who is among the living has hope' (verse 4). Even a living dog is better off than a dead lion. It's such a stark way of putting it, but the point is simple: to be alive is to have the day of opportunity in our hands in a way that we do not have when we're dead. That's the point of verses 5–6. The time is coming when all the things you think are the most important in the world, all your strongest emotions – your love, your hate, your jealousy – the time is coming when they will all go cold and vanish and be forgotten.

In the end, death makes no sense. Death will leave your face tear-stained in perplexity. And because death is like that, then life works like this: God comes to us in Jesus and says, 'Trust me. Walk me with me. Love me. Put your hand in my hand. Believe my Word. Stop trying to understand everything, to be in control of everything, to tie up all the loose ends, to have perfect peace and wealth and health and happiness. Stop striving for all those things, and stop it now. If you can't see that life doesn't always make sense, then something is coming your way which will prove it to you. Death is coming.'

I am part of a younger generation which, as far as I can tell, has no conception of what it means to die well. Dying well doesn't mean that when death touches your family you do not have a broken heart. It doesn't mean that you do not experience suffocating grief. To die well means that I realize death is the limit God has placed on creatures who want to be gods. That includes me because, as my wife could tell you, I'm pretty keen on the idea of being the centre of the universe.

To die well means I realize death is not simply something that happens to me; it happens to me because I am a sinner. I realize that in a sense I cause my own death. To die well means I realize that every time I see a coffin, it preaches to me that the world is broken and fallen and under the curse of death – and I am a part of it. It means I realize that I am not owed three score years and ten by God. It is only because of his mercy that I am not consumed today. To die well means realizing that from the day I was born I lived under the sentence of death, and I am amazed that God spared me as long as he did. It means I have been heading for death from the moment I was born. It means I have been laying up treasure in heaven and that is where my heart is. To die well means everything I have in this world I hold with open hands because I love Jesus more than anything and anyone else and I'm happy to go home to him.

A good friend of mine lost his grown-up daughter to cancer. She was a strong Christian, and so is my friend. On one occasion, when she was dying, he was by her bedside in hospital when a friend of the family came to visit. This person happened to be a well-connected medical doctor who offered to see if he could arrange specialist help from Harley Street in London. My friend expressed his great gratitude for this offer of help, but then also said to the kind doctor, 'Remember, we all come to this.' As a father myself, it was so moving to see his profound grasp of reality in the face of his own daughter's imminent death. He was not being fatalistic or pessimistic. I know he longed for his daughter to be cured or healed, and he did not refuse the doctor's help. Yet my friend was living life by being prepared for death.

When confronted with death up close, everyone realizes that we all come to this. But if that is the first time it confronts us, then it will likely be utterly crushing. Realizing that we all come to this before we come to it is very different from only realizing it when it is staring you in the face.

But preparing to die, and to die well, does not mean drawing the curtains and dressing in black and thinking morbid thoughts. Preparing to die means thinking about how to live. But before we come to that, just look at the many things in life which are uncertain.

2 The many things in life which are uncertain (verses 11–12)

Here is the opposite extreme. We tend to live as if the one thing which is certain will never come, while the many things which are uncertain are certain.

Of course, maybe nine times out of ten the race is to the swift, and the battle is to the strong. The sensible person usually does know how to balance the budget and so there's food on the table. The brilliant normally do get the best-paid jobs, and the well-educated typically get the breaks. But not always. For 'time and chance happen to them all' (verse 11). The word 'chance' here is a bad translation; it's literally: 'time and happenings happen to all'. In other words, situations arise, circumstances change, unforeseen events occur.

That's why the betting industry usually leads to the bookies getting rich. You simply cannot predict what will happen, and where you think you can predict it, then the odds are short and there's no point putting money on it. But the one time when you do will probably be the one time the underdog wins and you lose out. You cannot know the future. Just like fish swimming happily along, or a bird landing for some food, then out the blue they're trapped and caught and they never saw it coming (verse 12). In exactly the same way, men and women often have their lives turned upside down by a disaster they never saw coming and which they always thought would happen to someone else.

As we grow up, we replace our childhood dreams of being a ballerina or a firefighter with hopes of an apprenticeship, or a degree, and a job, and a husband and children, and a house in a certain part of town with a big dining room where people can come and go and laugh and eat and talk together. You might simply long to grow old happily with your family and grandchildren around you. Ecclesiastes says maybe you will do all these things, or maybe you will be dead before the year ends. Maybe you'll never get that job. Maybe you'll get married and have kids, but never the house you want. Can you see what the Teacher is saying to us? Put your faith in something else that is not under the sun, because one event under the sun might change all your best-laid plans: 'No one knows when their hour will come.'

The Teacher of Ecclesiastes seems to have a twin brother in the New Testament, the apostle James. They certainly say the same kind of things:

> Now listen, you who say. 'Today or tomorrow we will go to this or that city, spend a year there, carry on business and make money.' Why, you do not even know what will happen tomorrow! What is your life? You are a mist that appears for a little while and then vanishes. Instead, you ought to say, 'If it is the Lord's will, we will live and do this or that.'
> (James 4:13–15)

So the question for us is: what does a life of beauty and meaning and purpose look like, poised as we are between these two extremes? On the one hand, my death is certain; on the other hand, the timing of my death is uncertain. So what should life in the meantime look like?

The answer the Teacher gives us here is not the kind of answer that you and I are very good at giving. His answer is very simple: life between now and then looks like a life lived well. If one day you will be dead, live today. If you do not know when you will be dead, live now, while you can.

The path of wisdom along life's road is to enjoy the gifts God has given you, the simple things that give you pleasure.

3 The simple things in life which are wise (verses 7–10)

Right at the start of verse 7 is a little word, 'Go'. We're not just told 'Eat your food with gladness', but 'Go'! Seize the day. In other words, set about it as if you mean it and know what you're about. Eat and drink with gladness and joy. The second half of verse 7 shows us that these things are a gift: 'for God has already approved what you do'. God takes pleasure in your pleasure. He's given it to you.

This is why we're touching the heart of Ecclesiastes. Gift, not gain, is your new motto. Life is not about the meaning that you can create for your own life, or the meaning that you can find in the universe by all your work and ambitions. You do not find meaning in life simply by finding a partner or having kids or being rich. You find meaning when you realize that God has given you life in his world and any one of those things as a gift to enjoy.

My mum still loves giving me Christmas presents. Every year it's the same. She asks me what I would like, and I say, 'Nothing thanks, Mum. I'm 40 plus; I don't need anything to open', and she gives me something to unwrap anyway. Even now, she just loves seeing her boys receive a gift from her. Any parent can understand this. Anyone who loves someone else can understand this. For what we love as we give is the pleasure on the face of the person who receives. The Teacher says that God is just like that. As he gives us gifts, it is a sign of his pleasure in us. When we enjoy his gifts, we are experiencing his favour. The only right way to respond to God's good gifts, and to his pleasure in giving us the gifts of food and wine and family, is to go and enjoy them.

'Always be clothed in white, and always anoint your head with oil' (verse 8). Sidney Greidanus points out that in the Bible, when people were distraught, they wore sackcloth and ashes to show their grief, but white clothes to reflect the heat of the sun, and oil to protect and nourish the skin, were worn to show joy and happiness.[1] Don't think that because you're going to die it doesn't matter how you dress or how you look. Rather, look after yourself. The world was meant to be a place of colour and life and beauty.

Enjoy life with your spouse, whom you love. Cherish and protect the person God has given you. If you're married, don't downplay this. We are not told: live with your wife or put up with your wife, but rather, enjoy life with your wife. If you are too busy to enjoy the life you have together, then you are too busy. End of story. If you do not enjoy each other, then it is likely that you are simply taking what you can from each other to pursue other goals and ambitions which are never going to give you all they promise. You may use each other to gain something that will turn out not to be gain – and lose each other in the process.

It's vital to see that eating, drinking, dressing and loving in these verses do not form an exhaustive list of God's gifts. Rather, it's a representative list of what it looks like to love life and to live it to the full. These things are a way of saying: when God made the world, he made it good, and no amount of being a Christian, being spiritual, ever changes the fact that God put you in a physical world with hands and food and drink and culture and relationships and beauty. Sin fractures everything, distorts everything. It means we cannot understand everything. But sin does not uncreate everything. So if we were to tap into the Teacher's world-view and train of thought, I think an expanded list would go something like this:

Ride a bike, see the Grand Canyon, go to the theatre, learn to make music, visit the sick, care for the dying, cook a meal, feed the hungry, watch a film, read a book, laugh with some friends until it makes you cry, play football, run a marathon, snorkel in the ocean, listen to Mozart, ring your parents, write a letter, play with your kids, spend your money, learn a language, plant a church, start a school, speak about Christ, travel to somewhere you've never been, adopt a child, give away your fortune and then some, shape someone else's life by laying down your own.[2]

You may be able to add to the above list in a hundred ways; I hope you can add at least a few more. Whatever your hand finds to do, do it with all you have. One day working and planning and knowledge and wisdom will cease, so do them now while you can. Dying people, who truly know they are dying, are among all people the most alive. They are not here to live for ever. They are here to live for now, for today – and most of all they are here to live with and for others.

This is just the way a wise old man speaks to a younger man. 'Ah,' he says, 'if I knew then what I know now, I'd do things differently. I'd slow down. I'd enjoy my kids. Only yesterday they were knee-high, and now they're gone. I'd take time to listen more than I speak.' The voice of experience speaks like that all the time, but here in Ecclesiastes God's voice says the same to us too.

It can, of course, be confusing when we try to work out how to put all of this intensely physical stuff together with being a Christian. What does it mean to love life and the world if it's passing away, and if I'm meant to enjoy God and live for Christ first and foremost? Let me say that the two things go hand in hand absolutely beautifully, and for this reason: in the created world, you can only truly enjoy what you do not worship.

The man who makes sex his God, and who worships it, discovers that actually what is normal, pleasurable soon becomes inadequate, not enough, and he becomes chained to a path whereby he begins to enjoy only perversion – which of course is no enjoyment. The woman who makes her family her God and who worships her children discovers that they fail her and disappoint her and do not achieve all that she wanted them to achieve, and so she is left empty and unfulfilled. You can fill in the blanks with every single one of the good things in this world that are listed above. When you worship God's gifts, they will never ever deliver what they promise, and instead will leave you empty and broken. As C. S. Lewis put it, 'Natural loves that are allowed to become gods do not remain loves. They are still called so, but can become in fact complicated forms of hatred.'[3]

But when we worship God and trust him and love him and walk with him, what we find is that he is not an old man in the sky who makes us bow down before him in a cold, white room, while he sits on a throne waiting to zap us when we get it wrong. No, what we discover is that God is like the host who welcomes us into his kingdom and to the most lavish of banquets for us to enjoy.

God uses different tools to make us homesick for heaven, and in this chapter he has set to work with some of them. Death and sickness and uncertainty and disaster and sorrow and grief – all of these are means God uses to dislodge us from seeking security here.

But so too are the gifts Gods gives. His gifts are also meant to make us homesick for heaven precisely because they're so good. I find it interesting that verses 7–10 are full of wedding imagery: food, drink, white, oil, a husband and a wife. That is because the Bible's picture of the best that life can offer us is simply a foretaste of a wedding banquet still to come, the beauty and grandeur and glory of which cannot be put into words.

It is not easy to tell exactly what the Teacher knew about the afterlife. As we have seen, he clearly believed in the reality of judgment after death. But it is striking that he makes so much of our eating and drinking in the present, when so many other parts of the Bible make just as much of our eating and drinking in the future. Isaiah 25 looks forward to the day when all God's people will eat a feast prepared by the Lord of 'the best of meats and the finest of wines' (verse 6). When that day comes, while we swallow the choicest of fare, God will 'swallow up death for ever' (verse 8). The book of Revelation looks forward to the marriage feast of the Lamb

(Revelation 19:6–10), and the Lord Jesus spoke about the coming great banquet of the kingdom of God (Luke 14:15–24).

But it is not that Jesus taught future feasting only. In David Ford's memorable phrase, 'Jesus literally ate his way through the Gospels.'[4] The sheer number of times Jesus and food are mentioned together is quite staggering. The reason is that he is the ultimate Teacher, the true wise man; he is the embodiment and fulfilment of the vision of life that the Teacher in Ecclesiastes has been holding out to us – God's good world is there to be enjoyed in relationship with others, and we eat and drink together now in anticipation of our feasting together then. Every meal is a foretaste, an appetizer, for the banquet yet to come.

It's why I think the title to Jeffrey Meyers' meditation on Ecclesiastes captures the book perfectly: *A Table in the Mist*. We eat and drink as we vanish from the earth like a vapour. But one day we will eat and drink in the city of the King, where death will have vanished from the earth for ever. We must never think that on the other side of death, in heaven, we will cast off this cumbersome physical existence to enter a higher plane of merely spiritual life. On the contrary, the Bible is clear that at the end the heavenly city comes down *to earth*, and in that new earth God lives with us for ever (Revelation 21:1–4). He will wipe away every tear from our eyes. Tears are as real and physical a thing as there can be.

At the end, in C. S. Lewis's words, we will not enter a spiritual world, but 'a deeper country'. In *The Last Battle* the children and the animals move from the old Narnia to the new Narnia, where they discover that 'every rock and flower and blade of grass looked as if it meant more'.

> It was the Unicorn who summed up what everyone was feeling. He stamped his right fore-hoof on the ground and neighed, and

then cried: 'I have come home at last! This is my real country! I belong here. This is the land I have been looking for all my life, though I never knew it till now. The reason why we loved the old Narnia is that it sometimes looked a little like this . . . Come further up, come further in!'[5]

Those without Christ often abandon themselves to eating and drinking because sometimes it looks as if that's all there is to do before we die. But those who love Christ cherish eating and drinking because it looks a little like what we will do after we die.

The gifts are from the real country. They smell and taste and feel like home.

Questions for discussion or personal reflection

1. Try to explain the message of Ecclesiastes in a few sentences.
2. What certainties do you rely on in your day-to-day life?
3. What strategies do you and people around you use to try to control the deep and profound uncertainties of life?
4. If our lives are finite, what impact should this have on our aspirations and dreams?
5. Try to say in your own words what it might look like to love life in this world even though the world is passing away.
6. What are some things you could actively seek to enjoy and relish today and tomorrow?

8

Things to know when you don't know

'Love God and do what you please.'
Augustine, *Homilies on the First Epistle of John*

Cast your bread upon the waters,
    for after many days you will find it again.
Give portions to seven, yes to eight,
    for you do not know what disaster may come
        upon the land.

If clouds are full of water,
    they pour rain on the earth.
Whether a tree falls to the south or to the north,
    in the place where it falls, there will it lie.
Whoever watches the wind will not plant;
    whoever looks at the clouds will not reap.

As you do not know the path of the wind,
    or how the body is formed in a mother's womb,
so you cannot understand the work of God,
    the Maker of all things.

Sow your seed in the morning,
>   and at evening let not your hands be idle,
> for you do not know which will succeed,
>   whether this or that,
>   or whether both will do equally well.

(Ecclesiastes 11:1–6)

Vantage point

Where do you stand to look at the world?

We all get our perspective from somewhere. What is it that gives you your perspective on life, on what you read in the paper and see on TV and what happens to you? From what standpoint do you process everything you see and experience?

It all depends, of course, on what we're talking about. We have different perspectives depending on what's in view. I think about football from the standpoint of being a Manchester United supporter. I look at food from the perspective of someone who loves eating it and hates cooking it. But then there are the important issues in life. What perspective should we adopt on death? What about life itself – how should we view it?

The Bible's wisdom literature is part of the means God uses to change our standpoint and radically shift our perspective as we look at the world. Left to our own devices, we think about life from the perspective of youth, beauty, success, career and personal happiness. Ecclesiastes, however, has been teaching us to think about life from the perspective of death. Stand by a graveside and learn how to live. Where should we stand to think about being young, and what it means to have potential and energy and vitality? We will see in the next chapter that the Teacher tells us to stand with the old and look at youth from that vantage point.

Ecclesiastes urges us to think about life under the sun from the perspective of life above the sun. There is a God in heaven, a wise and loving Father, who holds the righteous and the wise in his hands. Think about time from the standpoint of eternity. What you do, and how you do it, matters because God will bring everything and everyone to the Day of Judgment.

In chapter 11 the Teacher asks us: where do you stand to look at the things you don't know about life? What is your perspective on the things in your life that you cannot control? Now, everyone knows there are things we don't know. But the standard advice is to look at what is certain, to look at what we do know, and doing that will help us cope with what we do not know.

But the perspective of Ecclesiastes is different and counter-intuitive. The Teacher actually tells us to look at the things we know from the perspective of the things we don't know. Once we realize there are certain things we will never know, and once we realize we should stop trying to know them, it changes the way we think about the things we can know. The uncertainties of life are meant to have a shaping influence on the certainties of life.

This may sound complicated, but it is really very simple. Let's look at three things that we do not know, and then three things that we do know.

Three things we do not know

1 We do not know how to predict the future
In verses 1–2 we're told that we do not know the future. There's a strange picture of waterlogged bread and giving portions to seven and eight which we will come to in a moment, but for now, see the underlying note of uncertainty – you do not know what disaster may come upon the land.

With the next verses about clouds and trees and rain and wind and so on, the writer is telling us that while certain things are inevitable, and while we can read the signs and life normally follows a routine and pattern, ultimately we really don't know what will happen. We know it normally rains, but we cannot predict whether there'll be a flood.

'No one knows whether love or hate awaits them' (9:1). You simply cannot predict the future. Disaster strikes when we're not expecting it. On 1st April 2009 sixteen men boarded a helicopter in the North Sea to return to Aberdeen from an oil rig platform, and never made it home. It was a tragic accident which rocked the community where I live. Sometimes we get time to prepare for death – a long illness, and time to say goodbye; sometimes someone nips out to buy milk and disaster strikes.

We understand that we cannot know the future as a concept; yes, of course, it's obvious – but in reality, we often live as if the opposite is true. We have plans for this week; we have things in our diary for next month, the meal out, the weekend away, the visit of friends, and the parent council meeting. That's how we work and it's right and normal. But have you ever had in the back of your mind that you do not actually know whether those things will ever come? Probably not. Would realizing it make any difference to the way you go about your business?

2 We do not know how to do that which only God can do

Here is the second thing we don't know: 'you cannot understand the work of God, the Maker of all things' (verse 5). We don't know how to do what only God can do.

We can build our windfarms in the wide-open windy spaces, but can we actually see the path the wind takes? Do you know where it came from, how it was made, where it's going? We can get digital 3-D ultrasound images of a baby in the womb, but do we really know how cells divide at just the right time in just the right ways so that this part is a toe and that part is an ear? How does life actually begin?

The Teacher says that in all the work of humankind there are certain things only God knows how to do. We manage, but God actually makes. The same idea is most beautifully and powerfully expressed in Job, when God speaks to him out of a storm:

> Have you ever given orders to the morning,
>   or shown the dawn its place . . . ?
> What is the way to the abode of light?
>   And where does darkness reside?
> Can you take them to their places?
>   Do you know the paths to their dwellings? . . .
> Do you send the lightning bolts on their way?
>   Do they report to you, 'Here we are'?
> (Job 38:12, 19–20, 35)

The effect of all these rhetorical questions is that Job realizes that every time he answers, 'I don't know', God alone can answer, 'I know.' By taking him on a tour of the edges of the world and the heavens, God educates Job about the unfathomable depths of divine knowledge compared to what human beings can grasp with their tiny minds and faulty sense organs. God is asking Job, 'If you can't know what I know, how can you level charges against me based on what you know?'

Living under the sun, believers are happy to take comfort in knowing that they do not know. We learn, perhaps through great pain, to be deeply content with not knowing. To know all that there is about everything there is to know, to know it in all ways and at all the right times so that I have every bit of relevant data in front of me, well, that is the kind of control over the world that Ecclesiastes has been teaching me to surrender. I cannot know, and so I don't have to know. Trying to know, or pretending to know, is foolishness, not wisdom.

3 We do not know how to guarantee success and avoid failure
'You do not know which will succeed, / whether this or that' (verse 6). Being successful in what we do is probably one of our main goals in life. No one aims at failure. We want what we do to go well, to really mean something; we long to achieve certain things. And yet, ultimately, we do not know whether what we do will hit the mark and be accepted, or fall short and fail. The promising career path in the city, the right company, the right prospects – many embark on a great new venture only to find themselves without a job before they ever really got going. 'The best-laid plans of mice and men', and all of that.

Now what our Teacher wants us to do with these three things that we don't know is to keep hold of them as we walk over to where he is, take them on to his vantage point for looking at the world, and let them teach us some wisdom. From the standpoint of your God-informed ignorance, now look again at the life you have and the things you do know.

Here's what we can see.

Three things we do know

1 Wise living means sitting loose to life and its possessions
Let's go back to the start of the chapter:

> Cast your bread upon the waters,
>   for after many days you will find it again.
> Give portions to seven, yes to eight,
>   for you do not know what disaster may come upon the land.
> (verses 1–2)

These are rather cryptic verses, and there are as many opinions on what they mean as there are commentators. But I think there is a clue in the verbs which open each verse: 'Cast' or, literally, 'send out' your bread (verse 1), and then 'Give' (verse 2). I have bread and I am told to send it out; I have portions and I'm told to give them to seven, and to eight. These numbers are a way of saying that portions should be given generously. In the Bible, seven is the number of perfection, and so giving to seven and then to eight is giving completely, and then giving a bit more. Today we might say, 'Give portions to the *n*th degree.'

Now whether this is talking about business and commerce, like the sea-trade, or whether this is simply speaking about life in general, the idea is that because the future is uncertain, there is risk involved in what we do, but that risk is not meant to paralyse. Rather it is meant to free us to do what we do generously. You don't know what disaster will strike or when it will strike, so be as prepared for it as you can by giving and giving again, and sitting loose to what you have.

This is simply biblical wisdom. The Lord Jesus himself shows us this kind of wisdom by painting a graphic portrait of the kind of person who does not understand it. The person who does not sit loose to life's possessions is not wise. He is a fool:

> And he told them this parable: 'The ground of a certain rich man yielded an abundant harvest. He thought to himself, "What shall I do? I have no place to store my crops."
>
> 'Then he said, "This is what I'll do. I will tear down my barns and build bigger ones, and there I will store my surplus grain. And I'll say to myself, 'You have plenty of grain laid up for many years. Take life easy; eat, drink and be merry.'"

'But God said to him, "You fool! This very night your life will be demanded from you. Then who will get what you have prepared for yourself?"

'This is how it will be with whoever stores up things for themselves but is not rich toward God.'
(Luke 12:16–21)

One of the greatest mistakes we can ever make is to think about my life, my wealth, my possessions as if I can predict the future. You can't, says Jesus, so be rich towards God now, while you can. What's the point of your wealth if disaster next week might take it from you?

Notice how this works. It isn't simply a case of adopting a long-term perspective on the short-term. It is that, but it's so much more. Any financial advisor on the high street will tell you to adopt the long-term view. Any wise friend will remind you that the future is uncertain and so you should distribute risk by not putting all your eggs in one basket. And some people will say, 'The future is uncertain, so eat dessert first. You may not live to eighty, so why save and save and save? Spend now and enjoy it while you can.' But here's what Ecclesiastes is saying: 'The future is uncertain, so give your dessert away. Give it away. Sit loose to life by giving your life away. Sit loose to your possessions by giving them away.'[1]

The Teacher of Ecclesiastes is talking about wise generosity which takes action for the sake of others. It is an idea that receives beautiful development in the teaching of the Lord Jesus. 'Whoever wants to be my disciple must deny themselves and take up their cross and follow me. For whoever wants to save their life will lose it, but whoever loses their life for me and for the gospel will save it' (Mark 8:34–35). This is the back-to-front logic of life in Christ's kingdom: the way up to glory is the way down to suffering. The way to find is to lose. The way to get is to give. Jesus said of himself, 'now something greater than Solomon is here' (Luke 11:31). Jesus is the greatest wisdom teacher there ever was, not simply because he repeats the wisdom of Ecclesiastes, but because he actually does it: 'Very truly I tell you, unless a grain of wheat falls to the ground and dies, it remains only a single seed. But if it dies, it produces many seeds' (John 12:24). Jesus' own death was the ultimate giving away of life which gave life to others. And it is the pattern for our life: 'Anyone who loves their life will lose it, while anyone who hates their life in this world will keep it for eternal life' (John 12:25).

Here is wisdom you will not hear anywhere else: take the best of what you have and the best of what you are, and give them away. Hold them out in open hands to God and to others. Worldly wisdom builds bunkers and barns to prepare for disaster. Biblical wisdom instead throws open the windows and doors of our homes and builds schools and hospitals and churches, and sees rich Christians become much, much poorer than they might otherwise have been. Ecclesiastes-type wisdom, Christlike wisdom, grows believers who spend their life on living in the world, rather than on living in the world so as not to die.

To cast or send out, to give to the *n*th degree, costs. You'll know you're doing it if it costs. The way to begin to do it is to find the things in your heart that you think you cannot do without, and give them away.

Some of us hold our money very tightly. Panic and fear sets in when we see the savings dwindle. You can begin to prise your fingers open if you give money away, and as you give, you become rich to God. Others find it is our time. 'I need me time,' we say. 'I'm an introvert. I have to be alone to recharge.' Actually, what you will find if you start having others in your space is that you cope. You will not need an ambulance. The world does not end. You survive, and as you give to others who are more needy than you, as you die to yourself in the process, you will find that actually new life is growing in your heart. The kind of new life you weren't expecting or even looking for. The horizons of your world begin to expand. The things you think are most important begin to change.

The perspective of the Bible, the wise perspective – and it sounds so stark because we are so used to thinking in terms of predictability and ease and comfort and our right to life and happiness, and because we believe all these things more than we believe the Bible – is that you might be dead this time tomorrow.

If so, what would you wish you could have done with your money, your home, your time, your gifts – your life?

2 Wise living means that neither success nor failure is ultimate
There are better things to do than succeed, more important things to do than to make it in the world, and there are worse things to do than to fail. We long for success as one of the great desires of our heart: success in work, success in marriage, success in our hobbies, success in a happy retirement. Conversely, some of us fear failure with every fibre of our beings. To fail at something on a grand scale would be the worst thing that could ever happen to us. Being fired from work, redundancy, a failed exam, a negative review, an investment down the pan – and so our life goes down the pan too.

The Teacher is so wise about our love of success and our fear of failure. In verse 6 he is telling us that we should aim for success. The way to do that is by not being a one-trick pony. You don't know what will happen in life, so have two things up your sleeve, not one. You want the seed you sow in the morning to grow, but don't just watch DVD box sets every evening, because maybe the seed won't make it. This is the

Teacher telling us not to put all our eggs in one basket and to have different things on the go, so that if something fails over here, we will have something else going on over there. Success *is* better than failure. There's nothing innately good about inevitable failure.

Some people work while looking forwards all the time to retirement, yet when it actually comes, they hate it. Unbeknown to them, they have slowly bound up their whole identity with their work, and without it they become depressed and see no point to life. I think this danger is particularly acute for men. Most of us are very single track – work, work, work – home to relax, bed, do it all again. Ecclesiastes is reminding us that the world is bigger than we may realize. There is more than only one thing to do. Don't live entirely for only one thing, because when it fails, you might fail with it.

At the same time, what the Teacher is saying is deeper than this:

> If clouds are full of water,
>   they pour rain upon the earth.
> Whether a tree falls to the south or to the north,
>   in the place where it falls, there will it lie.
> Whoever watches the wind will not plant;
>   whoever looks at the clouds will not reap.
> (verses 3–4)

There is an inevitability to life – the clouds say it's going to rain. There is also a randomness to life – trees blow down here and there, and there's nothing we can do about it.

Some people see only inevitability. This is the way things are, and if we keep doing the right thing, success is guaranteed. Others tend to see only risks and the potential for failure, and so they don't do anything. But I think the Teacher is prodding us, again, with his one main message: the thing that is worse than either success or failure in life is failing to live in the first place. Paralysed by fear of failure, we never try anything. Driven by the desire to succeed, we focus on only one thing.

At the conclusion of the film *Braveheart*, William Wallace is preparing to face his executioners and is offered an anaesthetic by Princess Isabella of France to numb the pain of his imminent torture and death. He refuses to drink it.

'You will die; it will be awful,' she says.

'Every man dies,' replies Wallace. 'Not every man really lives.'

I wonder what difference it would make to your life if you believed that there were worse things than dying. What difference might it make if we really believed that it's worse to live in God's world in a way that is not really living? E. E. Cummings said that being undead isn't being alive. The Teacher is telling us that a life that depends only on success for its vitality and has no space for the unpredictable, or a life that shelters itself from the prospect of failure because it has space only for the predictable, is a kind of being undead, which isn't really being alive.

Life is gift, not gain. Give up your pursuit of profit from your toil and instead seek to enjoy the things that God has given you for what they are, and as you do that, you will know some reward. If what you seek to do is to control your life, to map it out and insulate yourself from all risk and all failure, then what you've forgotten is that you cannot control what only God can control. You will never know the delight of doing something that can give you back a reward that you weren't expecting.

'Remember this:' says the apostle Paul, 'whoever sows sparingly will also reap sparingly, and whoever sows generously will also reap generously' (2 Corinthians 9:6).

3 Wise living is its own reward

Although it is not explicit here in chapter 11, underlying these verses is the Teacher's belief that the reward of life is not located in the places where we so often assume it is.

We often think that we have our life, and God gives us his gifts, and we now have to use God's gifts to experience further rewards. So God gives us the gifts of food, drink, work and friendship, and we think we have to use those things to obtain extra rewards. We use work to get the gift of wealth or success. No, says the Teacher, your work is itself a gift simply to enjoy, regardless of whether it makes you rich or not. We use food and drink to fill our bellies and remove the discomfort so we can get on with what's really important in the day. No, the Teacher says again, slow down, have some friends round, open a nice bottle, savour what you're doing. Your friendships aren't there to bolster your confidence or your security or self-image so that you can now go and do something with your life. Don't use people like that; your friendships are themselves the gift.

A life fully lived is a life receiving the reward of today as a gift that you don't deserve and one that God has given you to enjoy. One day it won't be possible. Death is coming. So do your bucket list – not your to-do list. We all have a to-do list: feed the dog, go to the bank, do the shopping, phone the plumber. But Ecclesiastes is a book which urges us to do our bucket list.

If you don't have one, is it because you're too scared to have one in case it never happens and doesn't succeed?

If you have one, then do it. Make it happen, somehow.

You've got only one life. So live it.

Questions for discussion or personal reflection

1. What is your main vantage point for looking at life? Is it your own experience?
2. How much of your life is shaped by confident predictions about the future?
3. Do you shelter yourself from the fear of failure by having space only for the predictable in your life? Could you change this?
4. When was the last time you responded to someone close to you in a way which recognized that person as God's gift to you?
5. Is it new to you that God might not be against bucket lists? How can you do your bucket list and not lose sight of God while you do it?

9
One foot in the grave

> *'Inside every old person is a young person*
> *wondering what happened.'*
> Terry Pratchett, quoted in *The Times*

Light is sweet,
    and it pleases the eyes to see the sun.
However many years anyone may live,
    let them enjoy them all.
But let them remember the days of darkness,
    for there will be many.
    Everything to come is meaningless.

You who are young, be happy while you are young,
    and let your heart give you joy in the days of your youth.
Follow the ways of your heart
    and whatever your eyes see,
but know that for all these things
    God will bring you into judgment.
So then, banish anxiety from your heart
    and cast off the troubles of your body,
    for youth and vigour are meaningless.

Remember your Creator
    in the days of your youth,

before the days of trouble come
>   and the years approach when you will say,
>   'I find no pleasure in them' –
before the sun and the light
>   and the moon and the stars grow dark,
>   and the clouds return after the rain;
when the keepers of the house tremble,
>   and the strong men stoop,
when the grinders cease because they are few,
>   and those looking through the windows
>   grow dim;
when the doors to the street are closed
>   and the sound of grinding fades;
when people rise up at the sound of birds,
>   but all their songs grow faint;
when people are afraid of heights
>   and of dangers in the streets;
when the almond tree blossoms
>   and the grasshopper drags itself along
>   and desire no longer is stirred.
Then people go to their eternal home
>   and mourners go about the streets.

Remember him – before the silver cord is severed,
>   and the golden bowl is broken;
before the pitcher is shattered at the spring,
>   and the wheel broken at the well,
and the dust returns to the ground it came from,
>   and the spirit returns to God who gave it.

'Meaningless! Meaningless!' says the Teacher.
>   'Everything is meaningless!'
(Ecclesiastes 11:7 – 12:8)

Shrouded or shaped?

Growing old makes a body and an inner self part company, as one ages and the other stays young. It leaves a person depressed at the disconnect between the mirror and the mind – how we look to others versus how we think about ourselves – and generates denial as our limbs begin to do with difficulty the things they used to do with ease. This process leaves a person blinking in perplexity at the speed of life, which has hurtled towards its conclusion just as it seemed to really get going. Youthfulness leaves so quickly. And entering old age itself is to arrive in a season beset by all manner of difficulties, pains and sorrows.

Society deals with this inevitable decline in different ways. Western culture seeks to deny the reality of ageing in the marketing of beauty products, and the glorification of youth and beauty by affording great prestige to athletes in their prime.

There are also more extreme responses. In Las Vegas, the Cenegenics Medical Institute describes itself as the world's largest 'age-management practice'. For a very hefty fee, it aims to help you spend as long as possible in your body – it can feed you, exercise you, monitor you, drug you and adapt you to help you live as long as possible. In this world-view your body is the best thing you have, and you should aim to live in it as long as you can. Those who indulge in this pursuit seek to be 'amortals'. Rather than structuring their lives around the inevitability of death, 'they prefer to ignore it instead'.[1]

On the other hand, fine books and films face head-on the traumas of what it can mean to be alive, but physically deteriorating in mind and body. The 2001 film, *Iris*, depicted the ravages of dementia in the life of the British philosopher and novelist, Iris Murdoch. The film is so powerful because it shows her relationship with her husband, John Bayley, from its earliest days, through all the stages of her illness and decline. Julianne Moore, in *Still Alice*, deservedly won an Oscar for her heart-breaking portrayal of a brilliant professor left grappling with the effects of early onset Alzheimer's disease.

But there's also humour. Victor Meldrew of the television series *One Foot in the Grave* is a cantankerous old codger whose extreme grumpiness provides the humour of each episode. We never know what Meldrew was like as a young man, but we see him in his later years as resolutely joyless and intolerant, despairing about life and the way people are and, of course, it is always everyone else who is in the wrong. Always. The only vitality about him is the intensity of his annoyance and irritation at the state of the world. He has lost all sight of the goodness of life and the blessings it lavishes on him. He lives shrouded in death.

It should be no surprise by now that what I mean by this chapter's title is very different from the world-view of Victor Meldrew. Old age has made him the wrong kind of person, the kind who will never be happy until his one foot in the grave is joined by the other. Rather than living shrouded in death, Ecclesiastes has been teaching us to live shaped by death. It is bracingly realistic about the agonies of ageing and dying, but its realism does not go hand in hand with despair.

In the verses we will consider here, the Teacher's realism about being an old person leads him to issue commands to a young person. The coming failing of my body should inform the present working of my body. My certain death must invigorate my current life. Putting one foot in the grave is the way to plant the other on the path of life.

The Bible's realism about old age and death is both urgent – Rejoice! – and calm – Remember.

1 The urgent realism of rejoicing because judgment is coming

These verses are an overture to the epilogue of Ecclesiastes. They concentrate the book's central themes, but do so with powerful poetic beauty before the Teacher states his final conclusions in 12:8–14. Ecclesiastes opened with a poem about the cyclical pattern in nature and the world, and now it comes to a close with another poem about the universal pattern inherent in an individual life coming to its end. In chapter 1 generations come and go, but the earth remains for ever. Here in chapter 12 we see what that actually looks like, as the young become old and return to the dust of the earth.

It's important to observe that youth in this passage is a relative concept, for 11:8 says that enjoyment should be pursued throughout all of life, 'however many years anyone may live'. In fact, by 'young', the Teacher may mean anyone who has not yet entered the stage of life portrayed in 12:3–8, where body and mind are in decrepit decline. As we have seen throughout, the Teacher knows that this eventual return to dust is the reason to grab hold of life with both hands while the opportunity still exists.

Derek Kidner says that 11:7 is about 'the bliss of being alive'.[2] Importantly, it is the first of many creation images in this passage as we are introduced to the pleasures of the sun and light. The Teacher lets us feel the temperature of a beautiful summer's day wash over our bodies as we bask in its warmth. (Living in Aberdeen, Scotland, means that seeing the sun is not a daily occurrence. It is especially pleasing when it does come into view!) The Teacher is telling us, again, that the good God made a good world, and it is foolishness of the highest order to be blind to its goodness and shimmering glory as we live our lives.

But just as honeymoons are wasted on couples without children, so too, as the saying goes, youth is wasted on the young. They don't know how good they have it because their youthfulness is all they have known, and they unthinkingly assume it will last for ever. In 1827 William Hazlitt wrote an essay trying to capture what it *feels* like to be young, compared with feeling old. Death and old age, to the young, are 'words without meaning'. They are simply 'a dream, a fiction', and life is 'a delightful journey' with no end in sight 'to prospect after prospect'. Life is one big opportunity. 'To be young is to be as one of the Immortals.'[3] Being young feels like being unable to die.

We should note that the Teacher does not chide the young person in these verses for being young. His instruction is not 'You're young, but don't forget you'll one day be old', so much as 'You're young, so make the most of it with every fibre of your being.' To every person with the capacity to do so, in these words of the Teacher, God says, rejoice, be happy, find joy in the days when we can be physically, mentally and relationally active. God commands us: 'Follow the ways of your heart / and whatever your eyes see' (verse 9) – for one day the capacity, ability and desire to do so will all cease.

Here is where a huge surprise is waiting for us in this passage. Did you skim over the word 'command' in the paragraph above? You should have raised an eyebrow. Think of how we normally conceive of commands, and ask what it might mean that God *commands* joy and happiness and delight. They are not optional extras for the Christian believer living in the prime of life. Enjoyment is a command, and to break God's commands is always to trample his law and to invite his judgment. Does this sound right? Is God really this invested in your happiness?

Read verse 9 again, and notice the final part: 'but know that for all these things / God will bring you into judgment.' It is possible, of course, that the Teacher is telling us to go off and have fun, but, like a parent, is also telling us not to forget the curfew that could ensue should we come home late. He is certainly not encouraging licentious living and wanton abandon to the desires of our heart, for he has been too realistic throughout his book about what our hearts are really like. In verse 10 a more literal reading of the 'troubles' of the body which are to be cast off is that 'evil' is to be cast off. So it is possible that there is a reminder here that judgment awaits the pursuit of unwise and destructive pleasures. Be careful how you party!

But I do not think this is the best way to read the verse. It is much more likely that the Teacher is actually including our enjoyment of God's world, or lack of it, as one of the things that God will call to account in his final reckoning. We have already seen how enjoyment is a gift from God and, like all his other gifts, we are responsible to God for what we have done with it:

> Human beings are supposed to enjoy life to the full because that is their divinely assigned portion, and God calls one into account for failure to enjoy . . . enjoyment is not only permitted, it is commanded; it is not only an opportunity, it is a divine imperative.[4]

This means that pleasure is a divine decree that we ignore at our peril. For it is precisely in enjoying the world God has made that we show we have grasped the goodness of the God we say we love. Failure to enjoy is an offence, not merely an oversight. When the child does not enjoy the gift the parent has lavished on them, it is an affront to the parent's love as much as the child deliberately breaking the toy. No parent is glad that Buzz Lightyear sits pristinely in the box rather than being lovingly bashed and bumped in daily adventures. Real relationship involves seeing another person take pleasure in gifts given; delight is what we ask of the other as we freely give to them.

Although the analogy is not identical, God is like this too. It is striking that in Deuteronomy 28:47 Moses tells the people of Israel that the curses of the covenant will befall them, 'because you did not serve the LORD your God joyfully and gladly in the time of prosperity'. Christian living collapses when it is not delighted with the bounty God gives.

In a suggestively beautiful essay Douglas Jones argues that the reason Christian cultures have failed throughout church history is not primarily because of insufficient theological education, or poor doctrine, or inadequate evangelism, or weak leadership, but because of a lack of joy.[5] Jones reflects on Deuteronomy 27 – 30, which highlights the need for covenant faithfulness, but then he points out how in this passage we stumble across the need to be faithful in joy and gladness (Deuteronomy 28:47) and we are dumbstruck: 'Since when was that the pivot of reality? Certainly this has to be a divine typo.'[6] Jones shows how the joy the people of God were always meant to enjoy in the land is 'earthy joy', sheer delight in the gifts of food and drink and relationships and rest. It is when we enter into those pleasures that we resemble the trinitarian, self-giving love of God more than when we try to grow a culture based on duty and obedience. The more joyful we are, the more like God we are:

> The broad Christian community has many, many books on joy, but few of them appear to grasp the weight of joy. They tend to talk rather stoically about how to feel pleasure in the midst

of dysfunctional relationships. Joy is just a marginal psychological trait, not the center of the universe. How is it that, for centuries, Christendom can write creeds and theological tomes that don't tell us this simple point from Deuteronomy? Why haven't we had giant church councils on the nature of joy? Or different schools of thought that wrestle over the intricacies of joy? Why don't our creeds dedicate long sections to expositing the nature of joy for the people of God?[7]

In *The Screwtape Letters* the devilish writer cannot contain his disgust at the enemy's obsession with joy:

> He's a hedonist at heart. All those fasts and vigils and stakes and crosses are only a façade . . . Out at sea, out in his Sea, there is pleasure, and more pleasure . . . He has a bourgeois mind. He has filled his world full of pleasures. There are things for humans to do all day long without him minding in the least.[8]

Not to live gladly, joyfully, and not to drink deeply from the wells of abundant goodness which God has lavished on us, is sin, and it is a sin because it is a denial of who he is. It is a denial of God's covenant blessing. It is a repetition of the first sin, the primal sin of pride. Adam and Eve came to believe that God was withholding something good from them, and in taking it upon themselves to get it, they were charging God with not being good to them. In Kidner's wonderful phrase, 'This was the nerve the serpent had touched in Eden, to make even Paradise appear an insult.'[9] There is a way of looking at the world which sees God's goodness gifted to us and which causes us to live with constant wonder at his daily provision. There is another way of living which feels constantly slighted by God and others, and which becomes a greenhouse for bitter roots to flourish.

One day the extent to which we have embraced life's gifts will be called to account.

The thing to aim at in life is joy. I suspect that for many of us increasing our joy needs to start small before we consider going big by taking up skydiving or kite-surfing – although, for some, both things might be wonderful hobbies to pursue. We need to start small, because if we do not find joy in the little things of life, we are unlikely to find it in the big things. Let's start with gratitude.

In his two-volume biography of John Stott, Timothy Dudley-Smith records the words of one of Stott's study assistants who worked with him closely:

> Every afternoon at 4.30 pm I bring Uncle John a cup of coffee. As soon as I set the cup on his desk, he almost always says, somewhat playfully, 'I'm not worthy', usually without moving his bowed head from his papers. One afternoon last week I felt that it was particularly silly for him to equate worthiness with a cup of coffee. When he said, 'I'm not worthy', I responded, 'Sure you are.' After a few moments he said, 'You haven't got your theology of grace right.' I said back, 'It's only a cup of coffee, Uncle John.' As I went into his kitchen and began putting things away, I heard him mutter, still with his head bowed to his papers, 'It's just the thin end of the wedge.'[10]

When we are not grateful for the little things, it is only a very short step to no longer being grateful for anything. When we do not enjoy and savour and love and laugh and delight in the little things, then we are heading towards losing our delight in anything.

Victor Meldrew is a comic anti-hero, the exact opposite of the kind of person to be in old age precisely because he is grumpy rather than grateful. Grumpiness is a sin. It is, I think, particularly endemic among males. It is the kind of sin we tolerate and smile at, the kind we indulge as we return to the castle of our home and find it to be not completely to our liking. It is an emotion we cherish in our man caves at the twilight of a day ruined by interruptions and hassles or small children and annoying people. It is an attitude of heart and mind nurtured by the reign of self-pity, and from which the subjects of our self-made kingdom can suffer great harm because they have not treated us as we think we deserve. In the exercise of recalibrating your enjoyment in God's world, start with your heart. There is no point being like Bear Grylls in the forest at the weekend if living with you all year round is more like meeting the Gruffalo in the woods.

So start small if you need to. But wherever you start, do start somewhere. For the Teacher's realism about old age and death is what fuels the command to rejoice and 'let your heart give you joy'. It is a command infused with urgency because it can only apply 'while you are young'. One day things will change.

So ask yourself, is your future shaping your present?

2 The calm realism of remembering that life is for living

It is no coincidence that the Teacher tells the young person to remember their 'Creator' in the days of their youth (12:1), rather than simply telling them to remember 'God'. Ecclesiastes wants those of us who are young enough to hear him to realize that the doctrine of creation is the wellspring of a life well lived. It orients us to truths about God and about ourselves which can radically have an impact on how we live in the world.

Remembering your Creator means remembering that God made a good world, not an evil one, and that we are the ones responsible for spoiling it, not him. Remembering God as Creator means taking my place in the world in the appropriate way and not demanding for myself more than it is my right to have. Jacques Ellul comments,

> You may consider yourself autonomous, but you are incapable of knowing what should be done, incapable of knowing what wisdom is. You are a creature . . . Our problems do not stem from our failure to stay in our garden . . . All the evils, and I choose my words carefully, *all the evils of the world* stem from our taking ourselves to be the Creator.[11]

In the previous verse, the Teacher exhorted us to 'banish anxiety from [our] heart' (11:10) as we pursue joy and happiness in the world. If grumpiness grows with the sin of ingratitude, anxiety flourishes with the sin of idolatry. It is fertilized by the belief that I am in charge of my life and must do all I can to control my circumstances. On the contrary, as Jeffrey Meyers says, anxiety is actually the fool's response to the fact that his life is a breath: 'The fool has not rightly discerned his own vaporous existence. He is frustrated because he cannot manipulate existence to serve him.'[12] This is the exasperation of the would-be Creator discovering that he is, in fact, only a creature. The words of the Lord Jesus about anxiety sound just like the Teacher in Ecclesiastes. He too is reminding us that we are creatures, and God is the Creator who provides for our needs:

> Therefore I tell you, do not worry about your life, what you will eat or drink; or about your body, what you will wear. Is not life more than food, and the body more than clothes? Look at the birds of the air; they do not sow or reap or store away in barns, and yet your heavenly Father feeds them. Are you not much more

valuable than they? Can any one of you by worrying add a single hour to your life?

And why do you worry about clothes? See how the flowers of the field grow. They do not labour or spin. Yet I tell you that not even Solomon in all his splendour was dressed like one of these. If that is how God clothes the grass of the field, which is here today and tomorrow is thrown into the fire, will he not much more clothe you – you of little faith? So do not worry, saying, 'What shall we eat?' or 'What shall we drink?' or 'What shall we wear?' For the pagans run after all these things, and your heavenly Father knows that you need them. But seek first his kingdom and his righteousness, and all these things will be given to you as well. Therefore do not worry about tomorrow, for tomorrow will worry about itself. Each day has enough trouble of its own.
(Matthew 6:25–34)

The emphasis on creation in Ecclesiastes 11:7 – 12:8 also serves another purpose here. The call to remember our Creator while we are young is a command to recall how the world was meant to be, and to seek to live in the light of that, *before* the reality of how the world actually now is catches up with us and sweeps us along in the inevitable descent into old age. The fallenness of the created order has not removed all its goodness and beauty. If we live as if it has, then we have forgotten the Creator. The word 'before' appears three times: verse 1, verse 2, verse 6, and in verse 6 the refrain 'broken' occurs three times, each time referring to the final end of life in death. We must remember who God is, who we are, and how we should live, before the curtain comes down and the life we have been given by God is taken from us again by him.

Iain Provan points out that just as we have creation imagery throughout the passage – most strongly in verse 2 with the sun and the light, the moon and the stars, all echoing the creation story in Genesis 1 – so too the language of these things going dark refers to the 'unmaking of creation' as the good and right order of things is reversed.[13] Just as God made every person, so at the end, in old age and death, every person is unmade.

Consider the imagery in verse 2 of darkness and gathering clouds. Note the intensity of the picture: all the light-givers, sun *and* moon *and* stars go dark, and the rain does not give way to daylight, but only to threatening clouds. As Kidner says, it is a scene to bring home to us the 'general desolations of old age'. Not only may the lights of the faculties and the senses begin to fade, but so too the warm glow of old friends, familiar customs and long-held hopes. Age steals each away. He writes:

> All this will come at a stage when there is no longer the resilience of youth or the prospect of recovery to offset it. In one's early years, and the greater part of life, troubles and illnesses are chiefly set-backs, not disasters. One expects the sky to clear eventually. It is hard to adjust to the closing of that long chapter: to know that now, in the final stretch, there will be no improvement: the clouds will always gather again, and time will no longer heal, but kill.[14]

In the next verses the images change from meteorology to a domestic scene. We turn from the natural world's slide into darkness, to the fall of a great house into tragic disrepair. The Teacher uses the way in which a once magnificent building becomes dilapidated and ruined to depict what it is like to find your body failing with old age. It is a powerful collection of metaphors and allusions.

The 'keepers of the house', which now tremble, are your hands, once strong and capable of defending you and providing for others. Men in the gym nearly always focus on their arms, the place of strength. One day they will grow limp and begin to tremble. The 'strong men' now stooping are legs, no longer even able to bear your own weight. 'Grinders' are teeth, 'windows' are eyes, 'doors' are ears, and eventually they each fail, no longer able to chew sufficiently, or see completely, or hear perfectly.

Writing in the magazine *Vanity Fair* before his death from oesophageal cancer, Christopher Hitchens reflected poignantly on what it was like to lose the ability to speak. He came to see the essential link between speaking and writing – think of how a writer is encouraged to 'find your voice' – such that, 'To lose this ability is to be deprived of an entire range of faculty: it is assuredly to die more than a little.'[15] That is what the Teacher is picturing here. It is not just that these things are depressing in themselves, which they are; it is that they represent sad degeneration and decline from what once was. 'In the brave struggle to survive there is almost a more pointed reminder of decay than in a total ruin.'[16]

Old age brings with it light sleep and early waking, a fear of crashing to the ground, of the unknown and of venturing outdoors (verse 5). Hardly a day goes by when one of my children doesn't fall over and cut or bruise some part of their body, and yet it can all be laughed off or nursed away. They are young and vigorous; but a trip and a fall when you are old can spell disaster. Hair turns snow white: 'the almond tree blossoms'. The agile athlete who used to hop and skip and jump like a grasshopper has now slowed to an undignified Zimmer-frame shuffle. There isn't much appetite left for anything. With the failing body comes failing desire: he's back in the corner after lunch, snoozing again.

In Hazlitt's words, 'We do not die wholly at our deaths.'[17]

It all ends, of course, with a funeral. One day death arrives. The Teacher pictures light, provided by a precious golden lamp hanging by a silver thread. He imagines water, held in a vase provided by the pulley at the well (verse 6). Life is like the light and the water, and our bodies are like the lamp and thread and vase and wheel, encasing the precious commodities. The time will come when the vessel falls to the ground, and what it carries will ebb away. The body will break. Life will be over.

One day you will come undone. God's curse of creation in response to the fall means time will see you unmade. Maybe it will happen without the help of old age. It could come sooner rather than later. Or it may not begin to show for another thirty years. But the Teacher of Ecclesiastes is taking you by the hand and gently asking: before that day comes, how then will you live?

To sketch an answer, I want to close this chapter by providing in full a short piece by James Russell Miller, a Presbyterian pastor from the late nineteenth century who was also a prolific author. It comes from a collection of essays which Miller intended specifically for young people in his day.

His piece expresses better than I have been able to do here the essence of the Teacher's challenge in this part of Ecclesiastes. You will see immediately why it is so relevant. I have thought about all the individuals who first read his words and wondered what became of them as they grew old. Now it is our turn.

Beautiful Old Age
Softly, oh softly, the years have swept by thee,
Touching thee lightly with tenderest care;
Sorrow and care did they often bring nigh thee,
Yet they have left thee but beauty to wear.

This may scarcely seem a fitting theme to introduce in a book meant chiefly for the young, and yet a moment's reflection will show its appropriateness and practicalness.

Old age is the harvest of all the years that have gone before. It is the barn into which all the sheaves are gathered. It is the sea into which all the rills and rivers of life flow from their springs in the hills and valleys of youth and manhood. We are each, in all our earlier years, building the house in which we shall have to live when we grow old. And we may make it a prison or a palace. We may make it very beautiful, adorning it with taste and filling it with objects that will minister to our pleasure, comfort and power. We may cover the walls with lovely pictures. We may spread luxurious couches of ease on which to rest. We may lay up in store great supplies of provision upon which to feed in the days of hunger and feebleness. We may gather and pile away large bundles of wood to keep the fires blazing brightly in the long winter days and nights of old age.

Or we may make our house very gloomy. We may hang the chamber walls with horrid pictures, covering them with ghastly spectres that will look down upon us and haunt us, filling our souls with terror when we sit in the gathering darkness of life's nightfall. We may make beds of thorns to rest upon. We may lay up nothing to feed upon in the hunger and craving of declining years. We may have no fuel ready for winter fires.

We may plant roses to bloom about our doors and fragrant gardens to pour their perfumes about us, or we may sow weeds and briers to flaunt themselves in our faces as we sit in our doorways in the gloaming.

All old age is not beautiful. All old people are not happy. Some are very wretched, with hollow, sepulchral lives. Many an ancient palace was built over a dark dungeon. There were the marble walls that shone with dazzling splendour in the sunlight. There were the wide gilded chambers with their magnificent frescoes and their splendid adornments, the gaiety, the music and the revelry. But deep down beneath all this luxurious splendour and dazzling display was the dungeon filled with its unhappy victims, and up through the iron gratings came the sad groans and moanings of despair, echoing and reverberating through the gilded halls and ceiled chambers; and in this I see a picture of many an old age. It may have abundant comforts and much that tells of prosperity in an outward sense – wealth, honours, friends, the pomp and circumstance of greatness – but it is only a palace built over a gloomy dungeon of memory, up from whose deep and dark recesses come evermore voices of remorse and despair to sadden or embitter every hour and to cast shadows over every lovely picture and every bright scene.

It is possible to live so as to make old age very sad, and then it is possible to live so as to make it very beautiful. In going my rounds in the crowded city I came one day to a door where my ears were greeted with a great chorus of bird-songs. There were birds everywhere – in parlor, in dining-room, in bedchamber, in hall – and the whole house was filled with their joyful music. So may old age be. So it is for those who have lived aright. It is full of music. Every memory is a little snatch of song. The sweet bird-notes of heavenly peace sing everywhere, and the last days of life are its happiest days –

Rich in experience that angels might covet,
Rich in a faith that has grown with the years.

The important practical question is, How can we so live that our old age, when it comes, shall be beautiful and happy? It will not do to adjourn this question until the evening shadows are upon us. It will be too late to consider it. Consciously or unconsciously, we are every day helping to settle the question whether our old age shall be sweet and peaceful or bitter and wretched. It is worth our while, then, to think a little how to make sure of a happy old age.

We must live a useful life. Nothing good ever comes out of idleness or out of selfishness. The standing water stagnates and breeds decay and death. It is the running stream that keeps pure and sweet. The fruit of an idle life is never joy and peace. Years lived selfishly never become garden-spots in the field of memory. Happiness comes out of self-denial for the good of others. Sweet always are the memories of good deeds done and sacrifices made. Their incense, like heavenly perfume, comes floating up from the fields of toil and fills old age with holy fragrance. When one has lived to bless others, one has many grateful, loving friends whose affection proves a wondrous source of joy when the days of feebleness come. Bread cast upon waters is found again after many days.

I see some people who do not seem to want to make friends. They are unsocial, unsympathetic, cold, distant, disobliging, selfish. Others, again, make no effort to retain their friends. They cast them away for the slightest cause. But they are robbing their later years of joys they cannot afford to lose. If we would walk in the warmth of friendship's beams in the late evening-time, we must seek to make ourselves loyal and faithful friends in the hours that come before. This we can do by a ministry of kindness and self-forgetfulness. This was at least part of what our Lord meant in that counsel which falls so strangely on our ears until we understand it: 'Make to yourselves friends of the mammon of unrighteousness, that when ye fail, they may receive you into everlasting habitations.'

Again, we must live a pure and holy life. Every one carries in himself the sources of his own happiness or wretchedness. Circumstances have really very little to do with our inner experiences. It matters little in the determination of one's degree of enjoyment whether he live in a cottage or a palace. It is self, after all, that in largest measure gives color to our skies and the tone to the music we hear. A happy heart sees rainbows and brilliance everywhere, even in darkest clouds, and hears sweet strains of song even amid the loudest wailings of the storm;

and a sad heart, unhappy and discontented, sees spots in the sun, specks in the rarest fruits, and something with which to find fault in the most perfect of God's works, and hears discords and jarring notes in the heavenliest music. So it comes about that this whole question must be settled from within. The fountains rise in the heart itself. The old man, like the snail, carries his house on his back. He may change neighbours or homes or scenes or companions, but he cannot get away from himself and his own past. Sinful years put thorns in the pillow on which the head of old age rests. Lives of passion and evil store away bitter fountains from which the old man has to drink.

Sin may seem pleasant to us now, but we must not forget how it will appear when we get past it and turn to look back on it; especially must we keep in mind how it will seem from a dying pillow. Nothing brings such pure peace and quiet joy at the close as a well-lived past. We are every day laying up the food on which we must feed in the closing years. We are hanging up pictures about the walls of our hearts that we shall have to look at when we sit in the shadows. How important that we live pure and holy lives! Even forgiven sins will mar the peace of old age, for the ugly scars will remain.

Summing all up in one, only Christ can make any life, young or old, truly beautiful or truly happy. Only he can cure the heart's restless fever and give quietness and calmness. Only he can purify that sinful fountain within us, our corrupt nature, and make us holy. To have a peaceful and blessed ending to life, we must live it with Christ. Such a life grows brighter even to its close. Its last days are the sunniest and the sweetest. The more earth's joys fail, the nearer and more satisfying do the comforts become. The nests over which the wing of God droops, which in the bright summer days of prosperous strength lay hidden among the leaves, stand out uncovered in the days of decay and feebleness when the winter has stripped the branches bare. And for such a life death has no terrors. The tokens of its approach are but 'the land-birds lighting on the shrouds, telling the weary mariner that he is nearing the haven.' The end is but the touching of the weatherbeaten keel on the shore of glory.[18]

Questions for discussion or personal reflection

1. Reflect on your attitude to old age. How does Ecclesiastes challenge you?
2. If you are 'young', how can you 'remember your Creator'?
3. Is your future shaping your present? How do you know?
4. Is it a new idea to you that God has commanded enjoyment of the things he has given us?
5. What changes could you make to your life to 'follow the desires of your heart'?
6. If you are old, how can you rejoice in God's gifts and be thankful for gifts past?

10

Getting the point

'A book must be an axe for the frozen sea inside us.'
Kafka, letter to Oskar Pollak

Not only was the Teacher wise, but he also imparted knowledge to the people. He pondered and searched out and set in order many proverbs. The Teacher searched to find just the right words, and what he wrote was upright and true.

The words of the wise are like goads, their collected sayings like firmly embedded nails – given by one shepherd. Be warned, my son, of anything in addition to them.

Of making many books there is no end, and much study wearies the body.

Now all has been heard;
    here is the conclusion of the matter:
fear God and keep his commandments,
    for this is the duty of all mankind.
For God will bring every deed into judgment,
    including every hidden thing,
    whether it is good or evil.
(Ecclesiastes 12:9–14)

The wonderful work of words

They say that actions speak louder than words, and that a picture is worth a thousand words, but I'm not so sure. You might think I have to say that because I'm a preacher. Words are my work. I'm not denying, of course, the point those pithy sayings are making, but our lives would be empty and our relationships barren without the wonderful power of words.

Words do things.

When I preached through Ecclesiastes, I can vividly remember some of the congregation's facial expressions changing as they listened. It happens all the time as we interact with one another. The words we speak can make someone weep, blush, rage, or roar with laughter. Words birth emotions.

Words change things. 'Turn left,' the driving instructor says to the learner, and because of those words instructing the driver, the car changes direction. Words make things. When I meet with couples preparing to be married, they are immersed, naturally, in all the details of their big day (or at least one of them is). Their heads are spinning with seating plans and invitations and bridesmaids' dresses and menus. I try to get them thinking about the fact that while many different things may shape a wedding, it is words that shape a marriage. With two little words – 'I will' – they are going to change each other's lives for ever. Words of promise spoken in a wedding ceremony are not describing marriage, or commenting on it; they are creating it. Something exists after their words have been spoken which did not exist beforehand. Indeed, it is in our promising that creatures become most like the Creator. As Lewis Smedes says in a classic essay, only a promise 'affirms that the human romance will have a happy ending, and that the earth will be populated one day by a redeemed family living in justice and *shalom*'.[1] Human destiny rests on a word of divine promise.

Words can wound, and words can heal. Words are weapons, and words are wine.

I love you.

I hate you.

I never want to see you again.

I forgive you.

I cannot forgive you.

You're my best friend.

I'm sorry.

It's because of what words do that we have the book of Ecclesiastes. God gave us words because he loves creating things. He loves changing things. He loves seeing something come into being that didn't exist beforehand. He spoke – just opened his mouth, and angels shouted for joy as the universe was born – and with a word, he created everything. Just as he spoke like that, so he speaks here, now, in these words, so that something will happen to us as we hear them.

Why didn't God reveal himself to us in a picture book? Why didn't Jesus enter the world at a time when he could be recorded and put on YouTube? If you sit with a child and read a picture-book Bible, made up only of images and no words at all, you will find that you cannot flick the pages without opening your mouth. It happens subconsciously, and you find yourself pointing and explaining. Images need interpreting. Actions without words only make sense in a context that has actually been created by words. So it is that God has given words from him, about him, for us. Revelation of himself is at the heart of who God is. 'In the beginning was the Word' (John 1:1). It's why Ecclesiastes has shown us that the primary sense organs of Christian faith are our ears. To know God, we need to be able to hear him.

This conclusion to Ecclesiastes is where the Teacher sits us down and one last time tells us to be sure we understand how his words work. In the previous chapter he answered a question about timing for us. *When* should I remember my Creator? Before it's too late, in the days of my youth. Now, in this final section, he is answering two more questions: *how* do I remember my Creator, and *why* should I remember my Creator? How and why should I live wisely in God's world?

The Teacher concludes by reminding us about his message throughout the whole book of Ecclesiastes. Verses 9–12 provide a mini-commentary on his book. These verses explain how and why the wise Teacher did what he did with words, and they explain what their intended effect is on us.

He wasn't an ivory-tower scholar, shut away in the university library with his books, and thinking that because he was reading and reading he was getting wiser and wiser. He was wise, that's true, but 'he imparted knowledge to the people' (verse 9). He shared it. He used his wisdom to make others wise. He looked at life and saw that often little pithy sayings, proverbs, perfectly captured the complexity and bewilderment of life, and he wrote them down. He studied people and situations and events, in all their regularity and randomness, and wrote down what he observed.

He finishes by telling us that these observations are meant to bring us four things. The Teacher's reflection on his book will enable us to reflect on what we have seen throughout this book too.

Pleasure

It is a sad irony that many find Ecclesiastes to be a gloomy and pessimistic book, or are left unable to make any sense of it, when it was actually written to bring us pleasure. 'The Teacher searched to find just the right words, and what he wrote was upright and true' (verse 10). In fact, 'just the right words' is a very weak translation. A much better one might be to say that he searched to find 'words of delight' – words of pleasure – and because he had found such choice words, what he wrote was also upright and true.

How do you remember your Creator? How do you know that you know God? By listening to his words of delight and by finding them pleasurable. I hope that's something you have seen throughout this book. God is not a killjoy in the way he made the world. He is not a grumpy old man in how he wants us to live in the world, and he is not puritanical in the words he gave us to read which tell us about himself.

We often look at the Bible through the lens of the last word in verse 10: 'true'. We want to know if the Bible is reliable. Can we trust what it says? Is it true? That's fine. But the way the Bible actually works is by being beautiful because it is true, and by being true because it is beautiful.

I have a friend who dislikes the gospel of the Lord Jesus and hates the idea that God might have anything to do with his life. He often mocks the Bible: it's antiquated, out of date, boring, irrelevant, and belongs in the Victorian era. What it says does not seem beautiful to him and it is not true. And yet much about my friend's life is a mess. He basically lives for himself, and because he does so, his relationships quickly become distorted and even destructive, and much of life becomes emotionally chaotic. He alternates between trying to insulate himself from others and trying to connect with others, but without any deep willingness to commit to others. Without the Bible's truth in his life, there is also an absence of beauty. Without the Bible's conception of pleasure, he has to construct his own, and it will always be driven by a selfish understanding of pleasure which will constantly narrow in around himself.

What God gives us in the Bible are words of delight that tell us by the very way in which they are delightful what is true. It's one thing to say you need to remember God before the day of trouble and old age, but it's quite another to urge us to remember him 'before the silver cord is severed' or 'the golden bowl is broken; / before the pitcher is shattered at the spring / and the wheel broken at the well' (12:6). The poetry about old age being like a house that is closing down makes us feel the poignancy of old age, and by its very form drives home the urgency of knowing God now, while we can.

That is how so much of the Bible works. Now that you're about to finish Ecclesiastes, read on into Song of Songs. It's one thing for God to tell us what marriage is – one man, one woman, joined together – but quite another for him to give us poetry to express what it's like to be in love and to make love. The truth of the words is not detachable from the beauty of the words. Read Job 38 – 41, Psalm 23, Isaiah 40 and 65, Luke 7:36–50, and Revelation 21 – 22, to name just a few of my own favourite passages.

You know your Creator when you realize that the words he speaks are meant to make you smile. But another way to know that you know God is when what he says also makes you wince.

Pain

'The words of the wise are like goads, their collected sayings like firmly embedded nails – given by one shepherd' (verse 11). Goads were employed by herd drivers in the ancient world to keep animals on a straight path. They were staffs with sharp nails embedded in them, and were used to poke and prod the animal. If it went to the left, there would be pain; if it went to the right, pain; if it stopped, more pain. The only way not to get hurt was to go the way the shepherd wanted the animal to go.

The Teacher's words are like nails. They wound. Some of them may have come to you with a very sharp tip indeed. But they have come to you directly from God, from the one Shepherd. It may be hard to learn that if you want to know and love and walk with God all your days, then what you will need is some pain. Some words to make you sit up and take notice. Words to stop you in your tracks, and to turn you around and get you going in the right direction:

> And I declared that the dead,
>   who had already died,
> are happier than the living,
>   who are still alive.
>
> (4:2)

> A good name is better than fine perfume,
>   and the day of death better than the day of birth.
>
> (7:1)

> However many years anyone may live,
>   let them enjoy them all.
> But let them remember the days of darkness,
>   for there will be many.
>   Everything to come is meaningless.
>
> (11:8)

You are going to die.

We wince.

These are sharp words from a loving Shepherd. That means we are sheep. These farm animals are not known for being the brightest in the world. They need a sheepdog. They need a shepherd. We need all the help we can get to keep going in a straight line.

God gave Adam and Eve the path to life, a straight line to walk in, and they veered off to the left to graze on different food. God shows us the path to life in his Word, a narrow way to walk in with Christ as our King – and we veer off to the right to graze for a while. I'm young, everything's fine, it always happens to someone else. I'll be grand.

Remember your Creator by letting his Word dispel your illusions and confronting your folly even if it hurts – and it may often hurt. Left to your own devices, you will not choose what is right. Left to wander along myself, I'll end up going in the opposite direction to where I should be. There is no sat nav for our souls other than the words from our one Shepherd. The Bible is supreme.

I want to suggest two ways to help you evaluate where you are in relation to these two things: the pleasure of the Bible and the pain of the Bible. They're attitude testers, ways of taking your own spiritual temperature.

First, you can measure whether you find the Bible delightful, not by how often you read it, or by how much of it you read, and not by whether you find it easy or difficult to read, but by whether you approach the Bible expecting to be surprised. Bible delight is born when you expect it to teach you something you did not know already. The more childlike you are towards the Bible, the more likely you are to find it having just the right words for you.

Marilynne Robinson is one of our finest living novelists. She has written three sumptuous novels, *Gilead*, *Home* and *Lila*, which I urge you to read some day if you haven't already. Put them on your bucket list. In a separate collection of essays she describes how she once found herself 'traveling all night to be home in time for church, and it occurred to me to consider in what spirit or out of what need I would do such a thing'. The reason, she says, is the magnetic pull of the Bible.

Robinson has been immersed in the Bible since her youth, and yet, 'I do not understand the Bible . . . By grace of my abiding ignorance, it is always new to me. I am never not instructed.'[2]

Now I am quite sure that Robinson and I would disagree about the Bible in all sorts of ways. Her beautiful novels contain so much of the Bible, yet leave me wishing for the inclusion of other themes that do not seem to register with her. I think there is more to the Bible in today's world than even she seems to grant. But what strikes me about what I quote above is that here is someone with a very fine mind saying she does not understand the Bible. She doesn't mean the Bible cannot be understood, but simply that because she comes to it with a certain view of herself, she is always expecting to learn. She is always expecting to hear something new. That is an attitude of the heart. It's childlike. She comes back to the Bible 'to have it opened for me again'.[3] I think we can learn from her approach to learning.

Listen to King David in Psalm 19:

The law of the LORD is perfect,
    reviving the soul.
The statutes of the LORD are trustworthy,
    making wise the simple.

The precepts of the LORD are right,
    giving joy to the heart.
The commands of the LORD are radiant,
    giving light to the eyes.

The fear of the LORD is pure,
    enduring for ever.
The decrees of the LORD are firm,
    and all of them are righteous.

> They are more precious than gold,
> > than much pure gold;
> they are sweeter than honey,
> > than honey from the honeycomb.
>
> (Psalm 19:7–10)

To speak like this requires a certain view of yourself. I am poor, so the Bible is precious. I am hungry, so the Bible is the sweetest of foods. I am unsure, disorientated and floundering, so the Bible is sure and trustworthy.

Second, a way to evaluate your relationship to the Bible's pain is to ask yourself when was the last time you submitted to it and acted on what it says, even when you did not like it. Have you ever obeyed it when you found what it was saying offensive? Reinterpreting the Bible to mean something different is always a moral exercise before it is ever an intellectual one. That is, if we do not like what the Bible says because it confronts us, then we will always find some way of changing what it means so that it now lines up with the world we want to live in instead.

Don't domesticate your Bible. Live in God's world – and realize that because we are sheep we will always, naturally, seek to develop our own goads to poke and prod the Bible instead of letting it painfully poke and prod us.

You will know that you know God when sometimes what he says makes you weep as he humbles your pride. Reverses your expectations. Upsets your priorities. Offends your behaviour. Challenges your thinking.

Perspective

Why should we delight in the Bible and allow it to wound us like this? One answer is this:

> Fear God and keep his commandments,
>> for this is the duty of mankind.
>
> (12:13)

What strikes me here is the comprehensive totality of the statement – my 'whole duty' – is to fear and to keep. This is the perspective to adopt on life.

We don't tend to think like that. We compartmentalize our life. We have hopes and dreams and aims and ambitions, and in the midst of that we think of our responsibilities to others: to spouses, children, parents, work colleagues, friends. But the Teacher reminds us that every single duty or responsibility we have towards anyone or anything else, we have towards God first and foremost.

Why do you need to be a certain kind of employee? Because you have to fear God and keep his commandments. Why do you have to be a certain kind of child? Because you fear God and know that he wants you to honour your parents. Everything I do for you, I do because I do it for God first and foremost: that's the kind of person Ecclesiastes is teaching me I ought to be. Perhaps if we were to think of doing everything for God first and foremost, it would quite radically change what we do for one another. It might make us bolder in what we say, more concerned for God's truth than one another's approval. It might make us more kind and more gentle, realizing that God has commanded us to forgive one another as he forgave us. It will make us more joyful, less grumpy and more generous. It will make us more alive.

Here is where the Teacher of Ecclesiastes lines up with the writer of the book of Proverbs: 'The fear of the LORD is the beginning of wisdom' (Proverbs 9:10). To fear the Lord is to remember the Creator, and vice versa, and this is the pathway to wise living. To fear and to remember is to regard God with all the adoration, love and obedience that rightfully belong to him. Charles Bridges says the fear of the Lord 'is that affectionate reverence, by which the child of God bends himself humbly and carefully to his Father's law'.[4] So fearing the Lord and remembering our Creator makes us wise, because it teaches us to live on our knees: it humbles us as the creature and exalts God as the Creator who knows what is best.

Preparation
As we have seen so many times, simple wisdom is preparing for the end:

> For God will bring every deed into judgment,
> > including every hidden thing,
> > whether it is good or evil.
>
> (verse 14)

One of the hardest things about Ecclesiastes is letting it instruct us that there are no immediate answers for some things in this life:

> I saw the tears of the oppressed –
> > and they have no comforter;
> power was on the side of their oppressors –
> > and they have no comforter.
>
> (4:1)

What do you say to that? What do you say to people who have experienced exactly those circumstances in life? There is ultimately only one answer – God will put it right. And we should prepare to meet him.

Some time ago I had a dream about a service I was going to lead at church. I dreamt that as I stood up to lead, I did not have the first clue what was happening. I didn't know what the songs were, what I was meant to be praying for, or what I was about to preach on. After the first hymn a few people simply got up and walked around, talking to one another. I gather it's quite a common type of dream – the fear of being unprepared for something major like an exam or an interview. It can be so disturbing – and then you wake up and realize everything is all right; you haven't missed the deadline; there is still time to get ready.

Ecclesiastes says that a day is coming when some people will discover that they are not ready for the most important event in the world. And it won't be a dream. Their life has been one long exercise in avoiding reality and ignoring what is coming towards them. For death and judgment are coming. The words of the Teacher are meant to be like the hand on the shoulder that rudely shakes us from our slumber and ends the dream, bringing us back down to earth with a bump.

But for the believer, death and judgment are not things to fear. They are a time when the terrors of this world will give way to the glory of the new world:

> No longer will evil be called good and good evil; no longer will darkness be turned into light and light into darkness; no longer will bitter be made sweet and sweet bitter (Isa. 5:20). The conflict between good and evil will come to an end, as will all arguments about motives, intentions, and the nature of good . . . Error will be exposed; real error, turning away from the Lord.[5]

It is so striking that while Ecclesiastes tells us there is no 'gain' to be had under the sun, the apostle Paul says that there is in fact one thing to gain: dying. 'For to me, to live is Christ and to die is gain' (Philippians 1:21). Paul knew that in Christ, living and dying means win-win. We can labour for Christ while we live, and we can live with Christ when we die.

Your death and the judgment to follow – the great fixed points of your life – are the very things that can reach back from the future into today and transform the life God has given you to live.

Questions for discussion or personal reflection

1. What is your view now of the book of Ecclesiastes? Has it altered now that you have reached the end of this book?
2. Pleasure, pain, perspective, preparation – which of these have made the biggest impression as you have read Ecclesiastes?
3. Do you approach the Bible expecting to be surprised?
4. When was the last time you submitted to what the Bible says even when you did not find it palatable?
5. What difference could it make to your life to realize that every duty you have towards someone else you have towards God first of all?
6. Are you preparing for judgment? What changes will you make to your life in the light of Ecclesiastes?

Notes

Preface

1. Christopher Hitchens, *Hitch-22: A Memoir* (Atlantic Books, 2010), p. 7.

1 Let's pretend

1. Ancient tradition held that the author of Ecclesiastes was King Solomon. This is widely doubted today, although I don't find many of the reasons for that doubt very convincing. It is interesting, however, that the book as we have it comes to us anonymously. We are simply told that these are the words of 'the Teacher'. So in keeping with Ecclesiastes' own self-presentation throughout this book, I will refer to the author simply as the 'Teacher', or the 'Preacher'.
2. Anthony C. Thiselton, 'Wisdom in the Jewish and Christian Scriptures: The Hebrew Bible and Judaism', *Theology* 114.3 (May/June 2011), pp. 163–172 (p. 165).
3. Peter J. Leithart, *Solomon among the Postmoderns* (Brazos Press, 2008), p. 69.
4. Iain Provan, *Ecclesiastes/Song of Songs*, The NIV Application Commentary (Zondervan, 2001), p. 56.
5. Graham Ogden, *Qoheleth* (JSOT Press, 1987), p. 32.
6. William Powers, *Hamlet's BlackBerry: A Practical Philosophy for Building a Good Life in the Digital Age* (HarperCollins, 2010), p. 79.

7. These were writing tablets which were 'pocket-sized almanacs or calendars that came with blank pages made of specially coated paper or parchment'. They were a technological advancement on the wax tablets that had existed for centuries (*Hamlet's BlackBerry*, pp. 145–146).
8. Leithart, *Solomon among the Postmoderns*, p. 100.
9. Douglas Wilson, *Joy at the End of the Tether: The Inscrutable Wisdom of Ecclesiastes* (Canon Press, 1999), p. 20.
10. C. S. Lewis, *The Screwtape Letters* (Fount, 1982), p. 107.
11. Ibid., p. 107.
12. Ibid., p. 107.
13. Ibid., p. 107.

2 Bursting the bubble

1. Iain Provan, *Ecclesiastes / Song of Songs*, The NIV Application Commentary (Zondervan, 2001), p. 56.
2. Douglas Wilson, *Joy at the End of the Tether: The Inscrutable Wisdom of Ecclesiastes* (Canon Press, 1999), p. 36.
3. Blaise Pascal, *Pascal's Pensées*, tr. W. F. Trotter (E. P. Dutton, 1958), p. 113.
4. Provan, *Ecclesiastes / Song of Songs*, pp. 83–84.
5. Ibid., p. 79.
6. Peter Kreeft, *Christianity for Modern Pagans: Pascal's Pensées, Edited, Outlined & Explained* (Ignatius Press, 1993), p. 172.
7. Ibid., p. 172.
8. Ibid., p. 187.
9. Blaise Pascal, *Pensées*, ed. Alban Krailsheimer (Penguin, 1966), p. 235.
10. Kreeft, *Christianity for Modern Pagans*, p. 169.
11. Jeffrey Meyers, *Ecclesiastes through New Eyes: A Table in the Mist* (Athanasius Press, 2007), p. 63.
12. Provan, *Ecclesiastes / Song of Songs*, pp. 74, 79.

3 Doing time

1. Iain Provan, *Ecclesiastes/Song of Songs*, The NIV Application Commentary (Zondervan, 2001), p. 87.
2. Ibid., p. 07.
3. Zack Eswine develops these things in characteristically thoughtful ways. See his *Recovering Eden: The Gospel According to Ecclesiastes* (P&R, 2014), pp. 130–135.
4. Craig G. Bartholomew, *Ecclesiastes*, Baker Commentary on the Old Testament (Baker Academic, 2009), pp. 180–181.
5. Bartholomew, *Ecclesiastes*, p. 179.
6. Eswine, *Recovering Eden*, p. 123.
7. Ibid., p. 130.

4 Living a life less upwardly mobile

1. I owe this point to Melvin Tinker, 'Evil, Evangelism and Ecclesiastes', *Themelios* 28.2 (Spring 2003), pp. 14–25.
2. Rebecca Konyndyk DeYoung, *Glittering Vices: A New Look at the Seven Deadly Sins and Their Remedies* (Brazos Press, 2009), p. 42.
3. Michael Horton, *Ordinary: Sustainable Faith in a Radical, Restless World* (Zondervan, 2014), p. 115.
4. Eugene Peterson, *The Pastor: A Memoir* (HarperCollins, 2011), pp. 130–142.
5. Jeremiah Burroughs, *The Rare Jewel of Christian Contentment*, abridged (Chapel Library, 2010), p. 12.
6. Douglas Wilson, *Joy at the End of the Tether: The Inscrutable Wisdom of Ecclesiastes* (Canon Press, 1999), p. 61.
7. Matt Chandler, 'Ecclesiastes – Part 6: Communal Lessons', sermon preached at The Village Church, 26 August 2006. Viewed online at: http://media.thevillagechurch.net/sermons/transcripts/200608270900HVWC21ASAAA_MattChandler_EcclesiastesPt6-CommunalLessons.pdf (accessed 4 September 2015).

5 Looking up, listening in

1. Iain Provan, *Ecclesiastes / Song of Songs*, The NIV Application Commentary (Zondervan, 2001), p. 117.

6 Learning to love the limitations of life

1. Gerald Sittser, *A Grace Disguised: How the Soul Grows through Loss* (Hodder & Stoughton, 1996).
2. Sittser, *A Grace Disguised*, Preface to the 2nd edn (Zondervan, 2004), p. 15.
3. Sittser, *A Grace Disguised*, 1st edn, p. 10.
4. Nicholas Wolterstorff, *Lament for a Son* (Eerdmans, 1987).
5. C. S. Lewis, 'The Weight of Glory', in *The Weight of Glory and Other Addresses* (Touchstone, 1975), p. 29.

7 From death to depth

1. Sidney Greidanus, *Preaching Christ from Ecclesiastes: Foundations for Expository Sermons* (Eerdmans, 2010), p. 233.
2. For an enjoyable and moving book-length portrait of this kind of life, see N. D. Wilson, *Death by Living* (Thomas Nelson, 2013).
3. C. S. Lewis, *The Four Loves* (Collins, 1963), p. 13.
4. D. E. Ford, *Self and Salvation: Being Transformed* (Cambridge University Press, 1999), p. 268; cited in Craig G. Bartholomew, *Ecclesiastes*, Baker Commentary on the Old Testament (Baker Academic, 2009), p. 98.
5. C. S. Lewis, *The Last Battle* (HarperCollins, 2010), p. 161.

8 Things to know when you don't know

1. I owe the language about what to do with dessert to Douglas Wilson, *Joy at the End of the Tether* (Canon Press, 1999), p. 111.

9 One foot in the grave

1. Catherine Mayer, 'Amortality: Why acting your age is a thing of the past', *TIME* Magazine (25 April 2011), p. 38.
2. Derek Kidner, *The Message of Ecclesiastes: A Time to Mourn and a Time to Dance*, The Bible Speaks Today (IVP, 1976), p. 98.
3. William Hazlitt, 'On the Feeling of Immortality in Youth', *Monthly Magazine* (March 1827), http://www.readbookonline.net/readOnLine/47762/ (accessed 10 August 2015).
4. C. L. Seow, *Ecclesiastes* (Doubleday, 1997), p. 371.
5. Douglas Jones, 'Revitalizing Reformed Culture', in Benjamin K. Wikner (ed.), *To You and Your Children: Examining the Biblical Doctrine of Covenant Succession* (Canon Press, 2005), pp. 207–224.
6. Ibid., p. 213.
7. Ibid., p. 213.
8. C. S. Lewis, *The Screwtape Letters* (Fount, 1982), pp. 95–96.
9. Derek Kidner, *Psalms 73–50*, Tyndale Old Testament Commentaries (IVP, 1975), p. 262.
10. Timothy Dudley-Smith, *John Stott: A Global Ministry* (IVP, 2001), p. 454.
11. Jacques Ellul, *The Reason for Being: A Meditation on Ecclesiastes* (Eerdmans, 1990), pp. 280–281.
12. Jeffrey Meyers, *Ecclesiastes through New Eyes: A Table in the Mist* (Athanasius Press, 2007), p. 208.
13. Iain Provan, *Ecclesiastes/Song of Songs*, The NIV Application Commentary (Zondervan, 2001), pp. 213–214.
14. Kidner, *Message of Ecclesiastes*, pp. 101–102.
15. Christopher Hitchens, 'Unspoken Truths', *Vanity Fair*, June 2011, http://www.vanityfair.com/news/2011/06/christopher-hitchens-unspoken-truths-201106 (accessed 10 August 2015).
16. Kidner, *Message of Ecclesiastes*, p. 102.

17. Hazlitt, 'On the Feeling of Immortality in Youth', *Monthly Magazine* (March 1827), http://www.readbookonline.net/readOnLine/47762/ (accessed 10 August 2015).
18. James Russell Miller, Chapter XXXI, in *Week-Day Religion* (Presbyterian Board of Publication, c.1880), pp. 300–307.

10 Getting the point

1. Lewis B. Smedes, 'Controlling the Unpredictable – The Power of Promising', *Christianity Today* (21 January 1983), http://www.christianitytoday.com/ct/2002/decemberweb-only/12-16-56.0.html (accessed 10 August 2015).
2. Marilynne Robinson, *The Death of Adam: Essays on Modern Thought* (Picador, 2005), pp. 230–231.
3. Ibid., p. 231.
4. Charles Bridges, *An Exposition of Proverbs* (Sovereign Grace Book Club, 1959), pp. 3–4.
5. G. C. Berkouwer, *The Return of Christ* (Eerdmans, 1972), p. 160, cited in Craig G. Bartholomew, *Ecclesiastes*, Baker Commentary on the Old Testament (Baker Academic, 2009), p. 294.